THE   RUSSIAN   JEWRY   READER

THE RUSSIAN JEWRY READER

Evan R. Chesler

*THE JEWISH CONCEPTS
AND ISSUES SERIES*

Published by
BEHRMAN HOUSE, INC. NEW YORK
in cooperation with
ANTI-DEFAMATION LEAGUE OF B'NAI B'RITH

ACKNOWLEDGMENTS

The editor and publisher thank the following for permission to reprint:

Crown Publishers Inc., for selection from *Teyve's Daughters* by Sholom Aleichem © 1949 by the children of Sholom Aleichem. Harper & Row Publishers, Inc., for selection from *The God That Failed* edited by Richard Crossman © 1949 by Richard Crossman. Holt, Rinehart and Winston, Inc., for selection from *The Jews of Silence* by Elie Wiesel © 1966 by Holt, Rinehart and Winston, Inc. *Keeping Posted* for charts appearing in December 1972 issue. © 1972 by The Union of American Hebrew Congregations. Little, Brown and Company for selection from *Khrushchev Remembers,* with an introduction, commentary, and notes by Edward Crankshaw. Translated and edited by Strobe Talbott © 1970 by Little, Brown and Company. Macmillan Publishing Co., Inc., for selection from *The Russian Jew under Tsars and Soviets* by Salo W. Baron © 1964 by Salo W. Baron. Macmillan Publishing Co., Inc., for selection from *The Great Terror* by Robert Conquest © 1968 by Robert Conquest. Macmillan, London and Basingstoke for selection from *The Bolshevic Revolution 1917-1923,* Volume I by E. H. Carr © 1968 by E. H. Carr. *Newsweek* for "The Leningrad Eleven" and "Nyet is No Answer" © 1970, 1971 by Newsweek, Inc. October House Inc., for "Babii Yar" by Yevgeny Yevtushenko from *The Poetry of Yevgeny Yevtushenko* edited, translated, with an introduction by George Reavey © 1965, 1967 by George Reavey. Oxford University Press for selections from "The Biro-Bodzhan Project 1927-1959" by Chimen Abramsky and "Jewish Religion in the Soviet Union" by Joshua Rothenberg both included in *The Jews In Soviet Russia Since 1917* edited by Lionel Kochan and published for the Institute of Jewish Affairs, London © 1970 Oxford University Press. S. G. Phillips, Inc., for selections from *The Collected Stories of Isaac Babel* © 1955 by S. G. Phillips, Inc. Praeger Publishers, Inc., for selections from *Russia under Khrushchev* edited by A. Brumberg © 1962 by A. Brumberg. Quadrangle Books, Inc., for selection from *The Unredeemed: Anti-Semitism in the Soviet Union* edited by Ronald Rubin © 1968 by R. Rubin. Random House, Inc., for selection from *The Basic Writings of Trotsky* edited by Irving Howe © 1963 by Irving Howe. Thomas Yoseloff for selection from *Star in Eclipse* by Joseph B. Schechtman © 1961 by Joseph B. Schechtman. *Time* for "A New Threat to the Detente." © 1973 by Time, Inc.

CONTENTS

UNIT II : THE SOVIET GOVERNMENT
DEALS WITH THE JEWS

UNIT III : SOVIET JEWRY TODAY

UNIT IV : THE FUTURE

MAPS

Introduction

Lev Davidovich Simonov is fourteen years old. He is a Jew and lives in Moscow. Davidovich is not really a middle name. It is called a "patronymic" and means that his father's name is David. Customarily, children are not called by their patronymics. Lev's family and friends usually call him by a nickname, "Lecha." Lev lives on Gorky Street in a three-room apartment with his parents, his sister, Nina, and his grandfather. The apartment consists of two bedrooms and a large sitting room. Lev and Nina share one bedroom, his parents have the other, and his grandfather sleeps on a bed in the corner of the sitting room. The apartment has no kitchen. The Simonovs share a "communal kitchen" with three other families on the floor of the apartment building. Each family has a special time for preparing meals and must be out in time for the next family's turn.

Lev's father works in a large paper mill as a cutter and binder. His mother is a clerk in the Commissariat (Department) of Housing. Nina is ten years old and attends the local primary school. Lev has just begun high school. Both he and his sister are members of the "Komsomól" (Young Communist

1

League). Although they had to join as part of their school requirements, they enjoy the activities of the Komsomol. The boys participate in camping and sports activities, much the same as the American Boy Scouts. The girls have many group activities, including sewing classes and sports.

By Soviet standards, the Simonovs live pretty well. They have an apartment in a fairly new building, enough clothes to wear (to save money, Lev's mother makes many of their clothes), and food for the table. Of course, some foods, such as fresh fruits and many fresh vegetables, are difficult to get. Much of the family's time is spent waiting on lines at food markets for different items. If Lev's mother hears that a supply of meat or vegetables has just come in, she hurries over to the market and waits on long lines with the other women to make her purchases. She must wait on one line to get the food and then on another to pay for it. If she must go to work or attend to some other errand, she often sends Lev or Nina to the food market to wait on line. But this is part of the life of most Soviet citizens, and it is taken for granted.

It seems, then, that the Simonovs have a good life. But when Lev was very young, about seven years old, he began to realize that his parents and grandfather were most unhappy. He often heard his father and grandfather talking late at night about their desire to leave Russia. At that time, he only under-stood that because they were Jews, the government often did not treat them fairly. As Lev grew older, his elders spoke more openly about the problems of the Jewish people in the Soviet Union. Lev was told that the government did many things to make life very difficult for Soviet Jews. He learned that his grandfather did not attend Rosh Hashanah services at the Moscow synagogue because government spies there wrote down the names of all the people present. Sometimes, these spies were members of the congregation who secretly worked for the government! Lev also learned that since the Soviet government considers Judaism a nationality, the passports of Soviet Jews are marked *Yevrei* (the Russian word for Jew). It made no difference whether a Jew came from the Ukraine, White Russia or Georgia; his passport would still read simply *Yevrei.*

As Lev approached the age at which he would enter high school, he became aware of anti-Jewish policies which directly affected him. In conversations with older Jewish boys, he learned that scores on high school entrance examinations were often lowered if the applicant was Jewish. Many of the older boys claimed that they could not attend certain special schools because their grades on the qualifying exams were too low. However, they had realized, by carefully checking the answers to the questions, that their scores should have been higher. Lev was also told that Jewish students were kept from attending the nation's major universities. The government had a "quota system," which meant that each university would accept only a small number of Jewish students each year. Once the quota was filled, no more Jews would be admitted that year.

Besides the problems Lev encountered at school, he was not permitted to obtain a religious education. Lev's father pointed out that religious training was prohibited for all religious groups. However, he emphasized that the Jews were subject to "special" treatment. While there is one church for every 2,000 Russian Orthodox persons and one house of prayer for every 10,000 Muslims in the Soviet Union, there is only one synagogue remaining in Russia for every 23,000 Jewish worshippers. His father also told him that the government prohibited the training of rabbis, the study of Hebrew, and attendance at religious schools. There were virtually no rabbis left in Moscow, and the few students who attended religious classes did so secretly. If they were discovered, they would probably be arrested. Because of these conditions Lev had never been inside a synagogue.

Lev now understood why his parents and his grandfather were so unhappy with their life in Russia. He understood, too, that he could never be happy if he were denied the freedom to worship as he desired, without fear of government repression against himself and his family. He firmly believed that he would have no real future in the Soviet Union. The only answer was to leave; to go somewhere that permitted a free and open life for Jews and for people of all religions.

THE "UNCHOSEN PEOPLE"

Indeed, the plight of Soviet Jewry has become a matter of worldwide concern. Jews in the Soviet Union do not have the right to freely practice their religion, or to provide religious instruction for their children. Most important, they do not have the right to leave the Soviet Union in order to find a place where they can live openly as Jews. While it is true that the general anti-religious policies of the Soviet government are directed at all groups in the country, the impact upon the Jews is often more severe. Perhaps this is due, in part, to the fact that the Jews are one of the few minorities in Russia without a separate Republic of their own. They are spread throughout the country, representing a minority of the population wherever they are found.

4

American newspapers frequently contain articles about the situation of the Jews in the U.S.S.R. Here are some excerpts:

Jews Reportedly Dispersed Outside Moscow Synagogue

Jewish sources said that Soviet policemen dispersed several hundred Jews from outside Moscow's main synagogue today after Sabbath services. . . . Policemen in much larger numbers dispersed more than 1,000 Moscow Jews from the street in front of the synagogue on the first night of Passover. . . .

In the crowd today were 37 young Latvian and Lithuanian Jews who had come to Moscow hoping for direct access to the authorities who they say are delaying their exit papers for Israel. . . .

A Baltic Jew said that five of the petitioners were threatened with criminal charges by the secret police if they continued what officials denounced as "anti-Soviet activity."

(*The New York Times,* April 2, 1972)

Soviet Playwright Expelled by Union

A Jewish playwright and songwriter has been expelled by the Moscow Writers Union on the ground that he encouraged Jews to

5

emigrate to Israel, informed sources disclosed today.

The sources, making available details on the union session last week, said that accusers at the meeting had addressed the playwright by his real name, as "Comrade Ginzburg," instead of his pen name, Aleksandr A. Galich. . . .

The nature of the accusations was not known last week, when the ouster by a vote of 15 to 4 was first reported. The action must be ratified by the national union, which action is expected to be a formality. . . .

Writers who are expelled from the union, which is an official professional organization, lose the right to be published.

(*The New York Times,* January 4, 1972)

Plight of Soviet Jews

Passover is the Jewish festival dedicated to freedom generally, and to the escape of the Jews under Moses from Egyptian captivity in particular. There is a special irony, therefore, to the reports from Moscow that on Passover eve this week the Soviet police strengthened their surveillance over the city's principal synagogue and broke up a crowd of young Jews congregating nearby.

A warning that something of the

sort might happen had been given several weeks earlier about the time that Soviet police in Kiev arrested eleven Jews for the "crime" of gathering outside the synagogue. Young Soviet Jews are apparently being informed by these tactics that they have no right to use the area near a synagogue as a meeting place, and that the synagogue is only for old people who wish to pray there.

This week, too, the Soviet Novosti news agency issued an extraordinary official statement on Jewish emigration. Apparently aimed at placating critics in the Arab states who have accused Moscow of providing Israel with military manpower by permitting some Jews to leave the country, the statement sought to minimize the extent of the emigration that has already taken place and to imply that there will be little additional emigration because so few Soviet Jews are interested.

These developments indicate the Kremlin feels itself to be caught between two fires, harassed by the pressure of the many Soviet Jews who want to leave and berated by Arabs who see Moscow playing a double game and helping Israel. Seeking a way out, the Kremlin is stepping up its intimidation of Soviet Jews while trying to mollify the Arabs.

But certainly for the foreseeable future the number of Soviet Jews going to Israel can hardly affect the military balance there significantly. Equally certain, emigration for those who wish is a basic right of all human beings, including Soviet Jews. President Nixon would do well to emphasize this point to Messrs. Brezhnev and Kosygin when he visits Moscow in May.

(*The New York Times,* editorial, April 1, 1972)

Scheuer Decries Ouster by Soviet

Representative James H. Scheuer, the Bronx Democrat expelled from the Soviet Union on the ground of "improper activities," said here tonight that his ouster was "pointless and irrational." The step apparently was designed to discourage Americans from private contacts with Soviet citizens.

Mr. Scheuer, who arrived here from Leningrad, denied that he had carried any material for distribution in the Soviet Union and that he had sought to encourage Soviet Jews to emigrate to Israel. He said he had three or four meetings with scientists who had been denied the right to emigrate but that such meetings "are not against the law."

"If you call sympathetic concern with the plight of such people as subversive activity, then I am guilty," he added in a telephone interview from his hotel.

Visited With Study Groups

Mr. Scheuer, who represents the heavily Jewish 22nd Congressional District in the Bronx, went to the Soviet Union as a member of a Congressional study group for a two-week tour of educational institutions. He remained there in a private capacity after the official tour ended Wednesday.

Explaining his private contacts, Mr. Scheuer said that he had carried with him the names of six or seven Jewish scientists denied permission to emigrate to Israel and the names of those Jews jailed after the Leningrad trials last year at which they were accused of having plotted to hijack a Soviet airliner. . . .

Mr. Scheuer said he hoped his expulsion would have no effect on the planned visit of President Nixon to Moscow in May. Any "escalation of the incident would be a monument to absurdity," he said.

Incident Not Stressed

He thus suggested agreement with the apparent decision by the administration not to build the incident into a major issue at a time when the United States and the Soviet Union are involved in a series of negotiations.

Mr. Scheuer, who is Jewish, said that he raised the plight of the scientists in a three-hour talk with Aleksandr B. Chakovsky, editor of Literaturnaya Gazeta. He said he also asked compassion for the women among the Soviet Jews imprisoned after the Leningrad trials, Sylva Zalmanson and Raiza Palatnik, who he said were seriously ill. According to the Congressman, Mr. Chakovsky agreed to look into the matter.

(*The New York Times,* January 16, 1972)

UNIT I : JEWS IN RUSSIA

CHAPTER ONE

Russian Jewry
Before 1850

It is difficult to say exactly when the Jews first moved from the area of the Mediterranean Sea to the region that we know as Russia. Ancient Greek writings mention Jewish settlements on the northern shore of the Black Sea in the first centuries of the Christian era. Some Jews travelled from countries in western Asia to the Caucasus Mountains at about the same time. The frequent wars between Rome (or sometimes Byzantium) and Persia led many Jews to flee to safer areas.

The most famous of the early Russian Jewish groups were the Khazars. The Khazars adopted Judaism in the eighth century. They lived in the southern portion of Russia, near what is called the Crimea today. It is possible that the Khazars chose Judaism because they wanted to remain neutral in the fighting which often took place between their Christian and Islamic neighbors. The Khazars brought rabbis to their land from western Asia to teach them about Jewish rituals.

The modern Russian empire is connected with the rise of "Kievan Russia" late in the tenth century, centered in the city of Kiev (which is today in the Ukraine). Prince Vladimir of Kiev chose to follow the Christian religion. There is a legend that he made this decision after talking with people of the Christian, Jewish and Islamic religions. According to the story, when Vladimir asked where the Jews live, the Jewish spokesmen replied:

> We do not live in Jerusalem, for the Lord was wroth with our forefathers, and scattered us all over the earth for our sins, while our land was given away to the Christians. Thereupon Vladimir exclaimed: How then dare you teach others, when you yourselves are rejected by God and scattered? If God loved you, you would not be dispersed in strange lands. Do you intend to inflict the same misfortune on me?

The emerging Russian civilization, with its newly-chosen Greek-Orthodox Christianity, was intolerant of any faith other than its own. Most of Russia's early religious leaders came from Byzantium, whose long tradition of religious intolerance included laws forbidding the practice of Judaism. But despite this anti-Jewish attitude, the Jewish community of Kievan Russia became quite prosperous. Although the Jews were apparently restricted to certain sections of Kiev, they became successful businessmen. The fact that many Jews were fairly well educated enabled them to exert a considerable influence on the Russian people. This influence was later to have a deep effect on the Church itself.

JUDAISM COMES TO MOSCOW

The center of Russian civilization gradually shifted from Kiev

14

to Moscow. By the thirteenth century, Kievan Russia had given way to "Muscovite Russia." The Jews had little influence in Moscow. In fact, the people of Moscow excluded most foreign groups, including the Jews. But Jewish influences came to Moscow in another way. Zechariah, a Kievan Jew, settled in the old city of Novgorod and began to spread religious propaganda. Because of his convincing arguments, a number of Novgorodian nobles and church leaders accepted some teachings of Judaism. Zechariah taught them that the Messiah had not yet come, and that it was idolatry to worship religious paintings and statues. A sect known as the "Judaizers" formed in the Russian Church, and began to spread its ideas to Moscow. Some sources indicate that even the daughter-in-law of the ruler of Moscow believed in the teachings of the Judaizers. But the leaders of the Moscow Church turned the people against this new sect, and many of its leaders were burned for the crime of heresy.

All during the sixteenth century, the rulers of Russia followed a severely anti-Jewish policy. Jews were often robbed of their possessions and forced to leave the Russian empire. When Ivan IV of Russia conquered certain areas, he forced the Jews living there to convert to Christianity. If they refused, they were drowned.

In the seventeenth century, Tsar Alexei brutally persecuted the Jews of Poland. He supported Cossack uprisings against Poland, and invaded certain portions of Poland and Lithuania. When his troops found large Jewish communities in these areas, Alexei tried to force the Jews to leave. Many of the Jews fled, hoping to find safety with the Polish armies. But before they reached the Poles, large numbers of them were massacred.

IS RUSSIA "READY" FOR THE JEWS?

Under the fairly enlightened regime of Peter the Great (1682–1725), the situation of the Jews was not truly improved. Peter felt that the Russian people were not yet ready for the admission of more Jews to Russia. When the mayor of Amsterdam suggested that many Jews be sent from Holland to Russia, Peter replied with this note:

> You know, my friend, the character and customs of the Jews; you also know the Russians. I, too, know them both, and believe me: the time has not yet come to unite these two peoples. Tell the Jews that I thank them for their offers and I understand the advantages I might have derived from them, but I would have pitied them for having to live among the Russians.

It is difficult to determine how Peter felt personally about the Jews. From what we can piece together, Peter the Great did not have personal anti-Jewish prejudices. He was perfectly willing to make close acquaintances with Jews, but usually requested that these Jews convert to Christianity. As Tsar of the Russians, he truly believed that Christianity was the only proper way to worship God. He wanted the men who served him personally to follow the Christian faith.

THE JEWS MUST LEAVE!

The plight of Russian Jewry seriously deteriorated in the regimes of Catherine I, Peter II, and Anna (first half of the eighteenth century). In 1727, all Jews were formally banished from the country. Most Jews moved westward, to Poland and the other nations of eastern Europe. Only in Smolensk, on the border between Russian territory and Poland, did some Jews remain within the empire. When one of these Jews erected a synagogue and converted a Russian man to Judaism, both the Jew and the converted Russian were brought to Moscow and burned in the public square.

The regime of Tsarina Elizabeth (1741–1762) was even worse for the Jews. In 1742, she issued an order in which she tried once more to expel the Jews from Russia:

> ... all Jews, male and female, of whatever occupation and standing shall, at the promulgation of this Our Ukase (Order) be immediately deported, together with all their property, from Our whole Empire, both from the Great Russian and Little Russian cities, villages, and hamlets. They shall henceforth not be admitted to Our Empire under any pretext and for any purpose, unless they be willing to adopt Christianity of the Greek persuasion. Such baptized persons shall be allowed to live in Our Empire, but not to leave the country.

THE JEWS BECOME RUSSIANS ONCE MORE

By the time of Catherine the Great (1762-1796), anti-Jewish prejudice was deeply rooted in the thinking of the Russian people. Catherine professed to believe that all people should be entitled to certain basic freedoms, but she had to be very careful when it came to discussing the Jews, because of the way most Russians felt about them. By Catherine's time most of the Russian Jews had either been massacred or had fled to

17

Poland. But now, through a series of wars, Catherine was able to carve up Poland and add certain formerly Polish areas to the Russian empire. Large numbers of Jews suddenly found themselves within the boundaries of that empire. Their freedom of movement was soon limited, and they were restricted to certain areas, the so-called "Pale of Settlement," within whose borders the Jews had to reside.

By the beginning of the nineteenth century, high officials in the Russian government began to realize that nothing would be gained by pushing the Jews out of the empire. Instead, they argued that the Jews might benefit the Russian people. Mikhail Speransky, a minister in the government, wrote in 1803:

> It is preferable and safer ... to propel the Jews toward perfection by opening to them new avenues for the pursuit of happiness, supervising their activities from a distance, and removing obstacles from their path, but without the use of force. One ought not to establish new special agencies acting in their behalf but rather encourage their own fruitful pursuits. In short, as few restrictions and as much freedom as possible − these are the simple ingredients of an effective social order.

Such ideas were aided by the then-popular concept of "mercantilism." This theory said a country should acquire undeveloped lands, from which they could get raw materials cheaply. These materials could then be made into finished products and sold, making the country rich and powerful. The Jews could help to develop Russia's industry because of their abilities in trading and business. So Jews were permitted to join associations of merchants and industrialists, and soon came to occupy important positions in Russia's business world.

But many developments which took place in those years harmed the Jews of Russia. For example, when a severe famine occurred in the western portions of the country in 1799, it was blamed on local Jewish innkeepers. The superstitious peasants rose up against the Jews, and killed many of them.

In response to the intense anti-Jewish feelings of the Russian people, the government adopted a policy of prohibiting Jewish movement within the country. Jews were forced to remain in those areas where they already lived. Jews were not permitted to leave the Pale of Settlement until the twentieth century.

In the early 1800s, Russia was ruled by Tsar Nicholas I whose motto was "Orthodoxy, Autocracy, and Nationality." In other words, Nicholas felt that the most important elements for a strong Russian nation were the Russian Orthodox Church, the unquestioned power of the tsar, and the protection of Russian national purity. There was no room in his Russia for "different" people, people of different religious faiths or national origins. In 1816, Nicholas wrote:

> The ruin of the peasants in these provinces are the Zhids (Jews) ... They are full-fledged leeches sucking up these unfortunate provinces to the point of exhaustion ... Surprisingly, however, in 1812 they were very loyal to us and assisted us in every possible way (in the war against France) even at the risk of their lives.

THE VICTIMS OF HATRED

It is easy to see that anti-Jewish feelings have been present throughout the course of Russian history. Superstition and prejudice are basically linked to the religion of the Russian

Church (known as the Greek Orthodox Church because it originally came from the Greek civilization of Eastern Europe). The Church has been the prime source of anti-Semitic teachings throughout Russian history. Its early leaders came from Byzantium, where Jewish religious practices had been outlawed. Anti-Jewish prejudice became a basic teaching in Russian religious circles.

But beyond this, a fundamental cause of Church anti-Semitism was the belief that the Jews were responsible for the crucifixion of Jesus. Perhaps you can understand how a Russian peasant might feel about the Jews when he was told that they were responsible for the death of Jesus.

In addition, the Russian peasantry formed anti-Semitic prejudices as a result of their everyday dealings with local Jews. Many Jews ran successful small businesses, and sold various supplies to the Russian peasantry. In bad years when the farms did not yield profits to the peasants they still had to buy clothing and food from the Jewish businessmen. This led to jealousy and hatred. Then, too, the Jews lived apart and followed Jewish religious customs. Some may say that the Jews remained apart from their Gentile neighbors because they were forced to. While this is certainly part of the answer, it is also true that the Jews wished to associate mainly with each other, and chose to stay away from much contact with the Gentile world. On both sides there was lack of knowledge of the other group, which resulted in feelings of distrust and suspicion of the unknown.

A GROUP WITHOUT A HOME

Still another factor served to single out the Jews of Russia for

21

THE   SOVIET   REPUBLICS

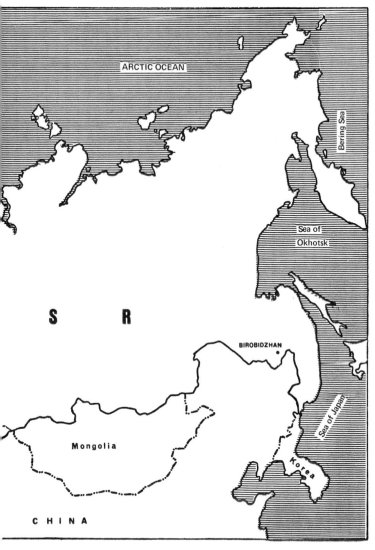

ARCTIC OCEAN

Bering Sea

Sea of Okhotsk

S   R

BIROBIDZHAN

Sea of Japan

Mongolia

Korea

C H I N A

1	Russian Republic (principally "Great Russians")	**8**	Georgian Republic
2	Ukrainian Republic	**9**	Armenian Republic
3	Estonian Republic	**10**	Azerbaijanian Republic
4	Latvian Republic	**11**	Turkmen Republic
5	Lithuanian Republic	**12**	Kazakh Republic
6	White Russian Republican (different from "Great Russlans")	**13**	Uzbek Republic
7	Moldavian Republic	**14**	Kirghiz Republic
		15	Tadzhik Republic

"special treatment." Nearly all of Russia's minority groups developed over the years within a specific land area. Looking at a map of Russia, you will see that the country is divided into sections, each of which bears the name of a national group. In general, when the government had to deal with any of the national groups within its borders it found itself concerned with a particular area of the country. Since the tsars wanted to avoid having one section of the empire cause trouble, or perhaps revolt, they treated each national group with a certain amount of care.

But the Jews, along with some other minorities such as the Gypsies, had no home territory. Instead, they were scattered among other national groups living in various areas. Jews in the Ukraine were surrounded by a majority of Ukrainians; Jews in Georgia lived among a majority of Georgians. Thus the government had no fears that strict measures taken against the Jews would arouse the antagonism of an entire region. This fact has been an important element in the persecution of Russian Jewry.

CHAPTER TWO

Russian Jewry in the Late Nineteenth Century

By the last quarter of the nineteenth century, Russia had become a restless nation. It had been under the control of the tsars for hundreds of years. During that time a small group enjoyed riches and privileges, while most of the people lived in terrible poverty. Decisions were made by the government with little or no regard for the common people.

For the Jews especially, the tsar's government was extremely oppressive. Jews were often blamed for Russia's problems and the people were encouraged to consider the Jews their enemies. The tsar himself donated large sums of money for the publication of anti-Semitic books and pamphlets which were widely read.

JEWISH REVOLUTIONARIES

Most Russian Jews believed that something had to be done to improve their lives, and many of them joined revolutionary groups. One such group was the Populists, who believed that the Russian peasants living in the countryside should overthrow the tsar. Jews joined the Populist movement thinking that if the government of Russia were changed, their life would surely improve. As Populists, they went out to the farms and talked to the peasants about how terrible conditions were in Russia and what changes could be made if only the tsar were overthrown. But they had little luck in convincing the peasants.

Many of the peasants were anti-Semitic. They believed that all Jews were wealthy businessmen who took advantage of the poor people. When anti-Jewish riots broke out, the non-Jewish members of the Populists did nothing to stop them. In fact, they encouraged the peasants to riot against the Jews in some areas. This was a great shock to the Jews who had joined the movement. Many of them agreed that some other group would have to be found to bring about the changes they desired. They could not, however, agree upon the revolutionary group which would best serve Russian Jewish needs. In fact, many Jews did not join any revolutionary movement. But nearly all the Jews agreed that something had to be done.

At the turn of the twentieth century Jews were barred from most important jobs, from the major universities, and from living among non-Jews. But the most dangerous threat to their existence in Russia was the *pogrom*.

THE KISHINEV POGROM

A pogrom was an armed attack on the Jewish section of a town, in which people were injured or killed, homes and businesses were looted and burned. There is little doubt that these pogroms were planned by the government. Sometimes Jews were blamed for a tragedy, such as a famine, and the local people "reacted" by attacking the Jewish section of the village. In other cases, the government would announce the beginning of a campaign to rid Russia of "undesirables" and pogroms would follow.

The following excerpt from *Free Russia,* a British magazine, describes a pogrom in the city of Kishinev in 1903.

The Massacre of Jews at Kishinev

Shortly before Easter, when the Bishop of the Greek Church in the Kishinev province was asked to contradict the absurd rumor . . . that the Jews murdered a young man for their ritual [at Passover] . . . this high priest publicly stated that he himself believed the story of Jews using Christian blood for ritualistic purposes.

The semi-official paper . . . openly preached the extermination of Jews for months . . . all applications for permission to publish a more impartial paper having been repeatedly refused . . . .

And still, when the actual massacres began, the Governor — it is said now — failed for two days to obtain orders from the Ministry and the Tsar at St. Petersburg to use military force against the housebreakers and murderers. Moreover, he refused in the course of those two days any communication with the suffering Jewish population (about 60,000 of the whole 110,000), never left his private quarters, closed all the telephones in the town to the public, and prohibited any private telegrams being sent from Kishinev to St. Petersburg.

The police of the town not only refused to render any efficient protection and assistance to the . . . attacked and murdered Jewish population, but deliberately prevented by force any assistance being rendered to them by those private persons who were willing to do so. The police actually pointed out Jewish houses to the rioters. Whenever Jews themselves attempted to gather and to show armed resistance, the police and military instantly attacked, disarmed, and dispersed them.

The results of this terrible circumstance are awful: 118 Jews, men, women and children, have already been buried, over 200 cases of serious injuries are still in the hospitals, and over 1000 cases of lighter injuries attended in infirmaries; 700 Jewish houses destroyed and demolished, 600 shops and stores broken into and looted; over 4000 Jewish families have been rendered homeless and destitute . . .

. . . It has been learned that there were about 12,000 troops in Kishinev at the time, against about 200 to 300 active rioters and house breakers. And as soon as the Government chose to proclaim martial law, after two days of delay, all disorders instantly stopped. Therefore, no one doubts in that part of Russia that this was merely a new tactical move of the despotic Government against the awakening people, and the Jewish movement in particular . . .

American newspapers carried frequent accounts of the pogrom in Kishinev. At first, the articles were simply announcements of what had taken place, such as this article from *The New York Times* of April 24, 1903:

Massacre of Jews in Russia

> **Twenty-five Killed and 275 Wounded in Anti-Semitic Riots in Bessarabia.**
> *St. Petersburg,* April 23
> Twenty-five Jews were killed and 275 were wounded, many of them mortally, in anti-Semitic

riots at Kishinev, capital of Bessarabia, on April 20, when a number of workmen organized an attack on the Jewish inhabitants.

The Minister of the Interior has ordered the adoption of special measures to restore order in the town and district.

A few weeks later American papers began to carry more detailed accounts of what had taken place. Many Americans were shocked by descriptions of the pogrom, such as this one, from *The New York Times* of May 11, 1903:

The Kishinev Outbreak

Russian Publication's Account of the Assault on Jews in Streets and Synagogues

The central committee for the relief of the Kishinev sufferers said in a statement issued last night. "The following from the St. Petersburg Vuedemosti is an answer to the Russian official denial of the anti-Jewish riots in Kishinev, offering a remarkable picture of the outbreak. The Vuedemosti is subjected to a strict censorship and therefore the account must be read in the light of what the Government permitted to be published before it decided that no riot had taken place."

The account published on April 24 said: "In Kishinev all was quiet until Easter Sunday when at noon the crowd on the Chuplinsky place, where amusement and other booths had been erected, became excited. Several Jews who came to watch the Christians enjoying themselves were attacked. They ran away. The cry 'Kill the Jews!' was raised, and the mob, which swelled instantly, followed in hot pursuit, particularly through Alexandrowsky Street to the new bazaar, where a fearful riot took place.

"It is impossible to account the amount of goods destroyed in a few hours. The 'hurrahs' of the rioters and the pitiful cries of the victims filled the air. Wherever a Jew was met he was savagely beaten into insensibility. One Jew was dragged from a street car and beaten until the mob thought he was dead. The air was filled with feathers from torn bedding. About 3 o'clock in the afternoon the rioters were signalling and whistling in the principal streets. The miscreants began there by breaking windows.

"At nightfall quiet was restored, at least in the centre of the city, and it was presumed that the disturbance was at an end. Police, troops, and mounted gendarmes patroled the streets, but the real assault only began on Monday morning, when, armed with axes and crowbars, the mob set upon its work of destruction, damaging the best houses and shops, clothing themselves in pillaged clothing and carrying away huge bundles of loot."

Editorials flooded the American papers denouncing the Russian government for permitting, and even encouraging, such atrocities. *The New York Times* warned the tsar's government that the United States would not stand for such senseless persecutions, and noted that America wished to open its doors to immigrants who came here of their own free will. While people who fled from oppression would not be turned away, the article claimed that the American government and the American people would register strong protests against the governments that caused such acts of brutality.

When the newspapers leaked the news that the government of Russia had encouraged the pogrom, the government arrested and brought many of the rioters to trial. In the trial, however, the lawyers for the rioters were not permitted to cross-examine witnesses. Two of the attorneys, M. Karabchevsky and M. Sokoloff, were deported to Siberia for their efforts to get at the truth during the trial. Here is an article about them from *The New York Times* of January 14, 1904:

> They were counsel for the rioters. Their defense was that their clients were poor, ignorant, slavish wretches who had been misled by the Government into doing what they had done. They had been led to think that they were pleasing the Government, or the local representatives thereof. There is every reason to believe that the defense was sound, that their crime had been connived at and instigated by the Government for the purpose of diverting their attention from their

31

own wretched plight, . . . To divert them, the Russian Government, through the famous circular of the Minister of the Interior, had advised the Local Government that the discontented Russians of Kishinev should be invited and encouraged to kill and plunder the local Jews. These bloody instructions had been carried out.

After the civilized world had begun to ring with execrations upon the massacre of Kishinev, the same bureaucracy which had instigated the massacre added the vices of hypocrisy and perfidy to the vices of cruelty and barbarity. It removed and disgraced the local Governor for doing what it had told him to do. It brought to trial the rioters for doing what it had instigated them to do. And when these brave lawyers attempted to prove the instigation the lawyers are banished to Siberia!

THE "NON-AFFILIATED" JEW

Not all Russian Jews were revolutionaries. Mainly, they were ordinary people, concerned with raising their children, making a living, going to synagogue, and getting some joy out of life. Indeed, many Jews did not understand the various revolutionary theories, for they were not politically inclined, nor did they feel the need to identify with the revolutionary groups, for there was no heritage of democratic government in Russia. Russian Jews were a peaceful people who wished only to be permitted to live their lives free from the complex influences of the outside world.

But their lives were devastated by the events which surrounded them. They were threatened by the pogroms, and challenged by the calls of the revolutionaries for sweeping changes in the life of the Russian people.

Perhaps the best known accounts of these people come from Sholom Aleichem, in his tales of Tevye, the poor Russian Jew. In one story, Tevye's daughter, Hodel, has just married Feferel, a revolutionary. Tevye speaks:

> There was only one thing I didn't like about [Feferel], and that was the way he had of suddenly disappearing. Without a warning he would get up and go off; we looked around, and there was no Feferel. When he came back I would ask, "Where were you, my fine-feathered friend?" And he wouldn't say a word . . . But you can say this for him: when he did start talking, you couldn't stop him . . . He had the wildest notions, the most peculiar ideas. Everything was upside down, topsy-turvy. For instance, according to his way of thinking, a poor man was far more important than a rich one, and if he happened to be a worker too, then he was really the brightest jewel in the diadem! . . . Money, he says, is the source of all falsehood, and as long as money amounts to something, nothing will ever be done in this world in the spirit of justice. . . .
>
> At the station I see a couple of young fellows, shabbily dressed, down-at-the-heels, coming to see my happy bridegroom off. One of them is dressed like a peasant with his blouse worn like a smock over his trousers. The two whisper together mysteriously for several minutes. "Look out, Tevye," I say to myself. "You have fallen among a band of horse-thieves, pickpockets, housebreakers or counterfeiters."

33

Coming home from Boiberik I can't keep still any longer and tell Hodel what I suspect. She bursts out laughing and tries to assure me that they were very honest young men, honorable men, whose whole life was devoted to the welfare of humanity; their own private welfare meant nothing to them. For instance, the one with his blouse over his trousers was a rich man's son. He had left his parents in Yehupetz and wouldn't take a penny from them. . .

"What good is your humanity and your workers," I say, "if it's all a secret? There is a proverb: 'Where there are secrets, there is knavery.' But tell me the truth now. Where did he go, and why?"

"I'll tell you anything," she says, "but not that. Better don't ask. Believe me, you'll find out yourself in good time. You'll hear the news — and maybe very soon — and good news at that. . ."

It was difficult for the average Jew to understand the beliefs of the revolutionaries. It was all too easy for him to understand the pogrom. Although the American newspapers considered such violence "senseless," the Russian Jew felt the brutality with all his senses. He was the object of a thousand years of prejudice in Russia, and he understood well the causes of the pogrom. Sholom Aleichem talks of it with almost startling humor.

This took place during the days of the Constitution when reprisals against the Jews were going on everywhere. Though I must tell you that we Jews of Heissin have never been afraid of pogroms. Why? Simply because there is no one in our town who can carry out a pogrom. Of course you can imagine that if we looked very hard we could find one or two volunteers who wouldn't deny themselves the pleasure of ventilating us a little, that is, breaking our bones or burning down our houses. For example, when reports of pogroms began drifting in, the few Squires, who are enemies of our people, wrote confidential letters to the proper authorities, saying it might be a good idea if "something were done" in Heissin also; but since there was no one here to do it, would they be so kind as to send help, in other words, would they dispatch some "people" as quickly as possible. . . And that was how the whole town became aware of the fact that a mob of hooligans was on the way, and that a plan for beating up Jews had been worked out. . . .

You can imagine what terror this struck in our hearts. Panic spread quickly. And among whom do you think it spread first? Among the poor, of course. It's a peculiar thing about poor people. When a rich man is afraid of a pogrom, you can understand why. He is afraid, poor fellow, that he will be turned into a pauper. But those of you who are already paupers, what are you afraid of? What have you got to lose? But you should have seen how they bundled up their children and packed up their belongings and began running hither and yon, looking for a place to hide. . . .

But a small minority of Russian Jewry felt that the oppression of the government and the hostility of their Gentile neighbors must be met with political activism. These Jews recognized the need for revolutionary struggle. It was only necessary to find the movement which could best serve the interests of the Russian Jews. Clearly, Populism had not been the answer. The following years would find Jews involved in a variety of revolutionary groups, all dedicated to bringing about change in Russia.

CHAPTER THREE

Russian Jewry in the Early Twentieth Century

THE ZIONISTS

In the early twentieth century, the Jewish community of Russia was divided into several groups. Some Jews, such as David Gryn (later known as David Ben-Gurion), joined Zionist organizations. Gryn was born on October 16, 1886 in Plonsk, a city in northern Poland, then under tsarist rule. His father, Avigdor Gryn, was a lawyer and ardent Zionist. David was brought up on Zionism. He considered Theodor Herzl, the founder of the international Zionist movement, to be one of the greatest men of his time.

Gryn and other Zionists believed that their problems could only be solved by founding an independent Jewish state in what was then called Palestine. They felt that since Palestine was the place where Jewish civilization originated, the land envisioned in the "biblical promise," it was the only real home the Jews could ever have. In the last years of the nineteenth century, Gryn helped to organize the Ezra Society to support

Zionism and the socialist pioneering idea in Palestine. This group was very active in teaching Hebrew to the people of Plonsk. In 1906, David Gryn left for Palestine to carry on Zionist work in the Promised Land.

THE BUND

Some Russian Jews, such as Victor Alter (of Polish birth) believed that the problems of Russian Jewry had to be solved in Russia itself. They were Jews, but they were also Russians and they wished to continue living in Russia.

The Jewish Workers' Bund was founded in 1897 and Alter came to it in the early part of the twentieth century when it was still a young organization.He envisioned the Bund as an organization comprised of Jewish workers, dedicated to changing Russia's system of government and at the same time protecting the interests of the Jews.

THE SOCIAL DEMOCRATS

Other Jews felt that there were better ways to attain true freedom for Russian Jewry. Julius Martov, for example, wished to join a group which consisted of many different nationalities, and which pledged itself to ridding Russia of all forms of prejudice. Martov came from a well-to-do family. His parents accepted many of the customs and beliefs of the non-Jewish Russian community. While a young university student, he became involved in illegal revolutionary activities, and was arrested several times by the tsar's secret police, but was released after brief sentences. Then he became involved in the Russian Social Democratic Party.

The Social Democrats called for the overthrow of the tsar, after which they claimed an "internationalist" society would be created. This society would join people together by economic class, and would not care what religions they practiced. But the Social Democrats soon divided into two groups, the Bolsheviks and the Mensheviks, because they differed on many issues, including the way in which the new government would come into being.

THE BOLSHEVIKS

Some years after the split of the Social Democrats, Lazar Kaganovich chose to follow the Bolsheviks (which means the "majority" in Russian). He was a Ukrainian Jew who became involved in the revolutionary movement at an early age. He quickly rose through the ranks of the movement in the Ukraine, and became an important figure in the government after the revolution in 1917. During the Stalin regime in the 1930s, he was put in charge of such programs as organizing farm workers and running the transit system in Moscow. In the years before the revolution Kaganovich believed that the tsar's government could only be overthrown by violent means. He, and the rest of the Bolsheviks, also believed that the party should be led by a small group of professional revolutionaries.

THE MENSHEVIKS

When the Social Democratic Party split. Julius Martov followed the Mensheviks ("minority" in Russian). He felt the party should be a large, popular group, which would be led by the people as a whole. Among the Social Democrats more Jews joined the Menshevik group than joined the Bolsheviks. Martov found himself surrounded by such well-known Jewish Socialists as Dan and Axelrod.

If these different groups disagreed in their ideas of how the new government of Russia should come into being, they all agreed that a change had to take place. Most of the Jewish Socialists mentioned above believed that all of the various groups would protect the rights of Russia's national minorities, including the Jews. But they were disappointed in 1913, when they read an essay written by a young Bolshevik named Stalin, entitled *Marxism and the National Question.*

THE HANDWRITING ON THE WALL: STALIN

Stalin had been asked by Lenin, the leader of the Bolsheviks, to write an article that would clearly state the Bolshevik position on the various minority groups living within the Russian empire. In the essay, Stalin argued that after the revolution, each national group would be permitted to have its own cultural and political institutions within the new state. Since each national group lived in a particular area, this idea was called "regional autonomy," or self-rule within a group's own region. However, Stalin argued, this concept did not apply to the Jews, because they were not a nation, and did not occupy any particular region within the empire. Rather, they were scattered throughout much of the country, and would

have to live by the rules and with the cultural institutions —
schools, newspapers, etc. — established by the dominant
nationality in the region in which they found themselves.
Stalin wrote:

> ... Of the five or six million Russian Jews only three to
> four per cent are connected with agriculture in any way.
> The remaining 96 per cent are employed in trade, industry,
> in urban institutions, and in general are town dwellers;
> moreover, they are spread all over Russia and do not
> constitute a majority in a single *gubernia* [region].
>
> Thus, interspersed as national minorities in areas
> inhabited by other nationalities, the Jews as a rule serve
> "foreign" nations as manufacturers and traders and as
> members of the liberal professions, naturally adapting
> themselves to the "foreign nations" in respect to language
> and so forth...
>
> The question of national autonomy for the Russian Jews
> consequently assumes a somewhat curious character:
> autonomy is being proposed for a nation whose future is
> denied and whose existence has still to be proved!
>
> ... In such cases [when a group is not really a nation] the
> advocates of national autonomy are obliged to foster and
> preserve all the peculiar features of a "nation," the bad as
> well as the good, just for the sake of "saving the nation"
> from assimilation, just for the sake of "preserving" it.
>
> That the Bund should adopt this dangerous path was
> inevitable. And it did adopt it. We are referring to the
> resolutions of recent conferences of the Bund on the
> question of the "Sabbath," "Yiddish," etc.
>
> Social Democracy strives to secure for all nations the
> right to use their native language. But that does not satisfy
> the Bund; it demands that "the right of the Jewish
> language" be championed...
>
> Social Democracy strives to secure the establishment of
> a compulsory weekly rest day. But that does not satisfy the

Bund: it demands that "by legislative means . . . the Jewish proletariat should be guaranteed the right to observe their Sabbath and be relieved of the obligation to observe another day."

It is to be expected that the Bund will take another "step forward" and demand the right to observe all the ancient Hebrew holidays. And if, to the misfortune of the Bund, the Jewish workers have discarded religious prejudices and do not want to observe them, the Bund, with its agitation in favor of "the right to the Sabbath," will remind them of the Sabbath. . .

Preservation of everything Jewish, conservation of all the national peculiarities of the Jews, even those that are patently noxious to the proletariat, isolation of the Jews from everything non-Jewish, even the establishment of special hospitals – that is the level to which the Bund has sunk!. . .

> (*Marxism and the National Question,* Chapter Five,
> "The Bund, its Nationalism and its Separatism")

Stalin went on to argue that the Bund was actually keeping the Jews from solving their problems. The real solution, he claimed, was for the Jews to assimilate, or "melt" into the larger society around them. They should adopt all of the customs and values of the Russian non-Jewish society, and then their problems would be solved. If they were truly part of the Russian society, they would benefit from the revolution exactly like all the other Russian people. Since they did not occupy their own territory, they could not possibly set up their own schools, newspapers and political institutions wherever they happened to live.

The Jews who read Stalin's pamphlet must surely have been

struck by his determination to see them give up their separate identity. But many recognized that Stalin represented only one viewpoint, and that the question of Jewish rights would have to be left until a new government was established, if that day ever came.

TO WHICH POLITICAL GROUPS
DID RUSSIAN JEWS BELONG?

1) *Jewish Workers' Bund* — was formed near the end of the nineteenth century by Jewish intellectuals and workers. The group believed that the tsar's government was not good for the working people and, specifically, for the working Jews of Russia. Its members felt that Jewish workers could best be represented by a Jewish organization close to the Yiddish-speaking masses. The Bund believed in maintaining separate cultural institutions for Jews, in order to preserve the Jewish people as a distinct group in Russia.

2) *Zionists* — believed that the future of Russian Jewry, and of world Jewry, depended upon the establishment of a Jewish homeland in Palestine. Beginning in the late nineteenth century, Zionist organizations attempted to convince Russian Jews that they could hope for no real future in Russia, even if a revolution took place.

3) *Mensheviks* — were one group in the Marxist Russian Social Democratic movement. (The other group was called the Bolsheviks, see above.) The Mensheviks believed that the

government of Russia had to be changed, and sought close cooperation with the organized workers. They also believed that their party had to be democratically structured, and made up of many people, from all walks of life.

4) *Bolsheviks* — believed that Russia's government could only be changed by violent revolution. They opposed the moderate tactics of the Mensheviks, and also opposed their ideas about the type of leading party Russia should have. The Bolsheviks believed that the party should be small, led by a group of trained revolutionaries.

5) *Non-affiliated Jews* — Many Jews were not really involved in the politics of the time. They were simple people, concerned with maintaining their families, and surviving the extreme hardships of life in Russia. Although they did not like the tsar, they were not willing to join revolutionary movements to overthrow him. These Jews were shoemakers, bakers, traders and farmers. In short, they were average people who did not have the time or any real desire to become involved in politics.

CHAPTER FOUR
The Revolution

In 1914, after a long series of minor political and military incidents, a major European war broke out. The western European democracies of Great Britain and France were allied with tsarist Russia against the central European powers of Germany and Austria-Hungary (the empire of Austria-Hungary was divided into the separate countries of Austria and Hungary after the war) in a conflict which came to be called the Great War (later, World War I).

The war inflicted terrible hardships on Russia. The tsar's army was not prepared for a major conflict, and there were serious shortages of food, clothing and ammunition. In a short time, these problems spread to the civilian population. Thousands of Russian people were without enough food and clothing. Although the Russian people had begun the war with great feelings of patriotism and loyalty toward the tsar, the extreme hardships resulting from the fighting quickly turned their enthusiasm to anger.

Despite the deep unrest among the civilian population and within the ranks of the army, the tsar did little to improve conditions. In fact, there was little that he could do, for Russian industry was not sufficiently developed to produce the tremendous amounts of supplies needed. However, the people were not satisfied with these explanations. They were hungry and cold, and tired of the injuries and deaths which war brings.

The widespread dissatisfaction was excellent fuel for socialist propaganda. All of the socialist groups discussed in the last chapter began to organize mass protests against the war and the food shortages. The Bolsheviks, for example, rallied many people to their side with their slogan, "Peace, Land and Bread!"

As the war dragged on into 1917, conditions worsened both at home and on the front lines. In the spring, mass riots broke out in several of Russia's cities. Taking this opportunity to move into action, a group of legislators demanded the abdication of the tsar, Nicholas II. The tsar was at the front with the Russian troops when he learned of the developments in Moscow and St. Petersburg. Since much of the army had transferred loyalty to the Duma (legislature) leaders, the tsar could not hold onto his office. He was forced to abdicate, in favor of his brother. But the tsar's brother refused to accept the post. Without a head of government and faced with violent rioting in the streets of the capital, the Duma leaders declared the formation of a Provisional Government. The government was to remain in power only until popular elections could be held.

A NEW GOVERNMENT FOR RUSSIA

Salo W. Baron, a noted authority on the history of this period, has discussed the first days of the provisional government, after the abdication of the tsar. In his book, *The Russian Jew Under Tsars and Soviets,* he wrote:

> With the majority of the Russian people and the subject nationalities, Jews welcomed with joy the so-called February Revolution of 1917. The government, first headed by Prince George E. Lvov and later by Alexander F. Kerensky, promised to introduce into Russia western democratic institutions based upon equality of all citizens and basic freedoms for both individuals and groups. On March 21 (April 3 on western calendars), 1917, a short time after the tsar's abdication, the Provisional Government published a decree removing all disabilities stemming from differences of race or religion. This meant that Jews were now equal citizens of the Empire.

Baron explains that all the organizations representing Jewish groups wished to get assurances from the new government that the rights of Russian Jewry would be protected. These organizations decided to call an all-Russian, democratically elected, Jewish Congress. A committee was formed which sent the following appeal to Jewish communities throughout Russia:

> Citizens, Jews! The Jewish people in Russia now faces an event which has no parallel in Jewish history for two thousand years. Not only has the Jew as an individual, as a citizen, acquired equality of rights — which has also happened in other countries — but the Jewish nation looks forward to the possibility of securing national rights. Never and nowhere have the Jews lived through such a serious, responsible moment as the present — responsible to the present and the future generations.

Unfortunately, the Congress of Jewish Organizations never met. Although the elections were held, the advances of the German enemy into Russian territory made an actual meeting impossible.

A SECOND REVOLUTION

The Provisional Government was not able to deal successfully with Russia's three main problems: bringing an end to the war, getting food for the starving masses, and transferring ownership of the land to the peasants. Because of its failure in these areas, the Provisional Government could not hold on to the reins of power. In October of 1917, the Bolsheviks were able to overthrow Kerensky's government with very little physical force. The takeover has often been called the "Bloodless Revolution" because so little violence took place.

A Bolshevik notice distributed throughout Moscow on October 25, 1917 announced the overthrow of the Provisional Government. It said, in part:

> The cause for which the people have fought, namely, the offer of a democratic peace, the abolition of landed proprietorship, workers' control over production, and the establishment of Soviet power — this cause has been secured. Long live the revolution of workers, soldiers and peasants!

In the first days of Bolshevik control, under the leadership of Vladimir Ilyich Lenin, there seemed to be reason for optimism among Russian Jewry. Although the Bolsheviks, following the teachings of Communism's founder, Karl Marx, were opposed to religion, they guaranteed freedom of religion in their constitution. They also guaranteed the freedom to oppose religion. E.H. Carr, in his book, *The Bolshevik Revolution, 1917-1923, vol. I,* describes the constitution as follows:

> The constitution began with general principles. The first four chapters recited . . . the Declaration of Rights of the Toiling and Exploited People. . . Chapter 5 enunciated a series of "general principles," including the federal character of the republic; the separation of church from state and school from church; freedom of speech, opinion and assembly for the workers, assured by placing at their disposal the technical means of producing papers, pamphlets and books as well as premises for meetings; the obligation for all citizens to work on the principle "he that does not work, neither shall he eat"; the obligation for all workers of military service in defence of the republic; the right of citizenship for all workers living on Russian territory, and of asylum for foreigners persecuted on the ground of political or religious offences; and the abolition of all discrimination on grounds of race or nationality.

A DREAM FULFILLED?

Those Jews who had joined the Bolshevik Party actively took part in the revolution which overthrew the Provisional Government. Although the Jews of the Menshevik Party were not directly involved in the revolution, they were well represented in the Duma at the time of the tsar's abdication, and played an important part in the affairs of the Provisional Government. Russian Jewry had long wished for a change in the government of Russia, and they clearly played an instrumental role in bringing about that change.

It is one of the strange facts of history, however, that the government which ultimately came to power in Russia soon took steps to rob Russian Jewry of its identity. The Soviet government's attempts to deal with the "Jewish problem" can be traced through the next fifty years of Russian history.

UNIT II :

THE SOVIET GOVERNMENT
DEALS WITH THE JEWS

CHAPTER FIVE
The Early 1920s

Within a very short time, the Bolshevik government began to view the Jews of Russia as a "problem" which had to be solved. Since the Jews had no territory of their own, the government felt they could not be treated like other groups. Moreover, the Jews had jobs which were often not acceptable to the new type of economic system the Bolsheviks wished to establish. Jews owned property, and ran their own businesses (food stores, clothing shops, etc.). These were economic activities which were opposed by the new government. A third factor in the "Jewish problem" was the anti-Semitism that had been a part of Russian history for so long, and that did not disappear with the revolution.

For all these reasons, the government undertook many different methods of dealing with the "Jewish problem." The government believed these actions were necessary because the Jews had persisted as a separate group throughout thousands of years of history, and it appeared that they would continue to do so. The Jews had always had their own newspapers, schools, synagogues and other institutions, and the government was not prepared to permit this type of separate existence. The Bolshevik leaders claimed that the only solution to the "Jewish problem" was for the Jews to assimilate into the larger Russian society. Yet, at the same time, they tried to single out the Jews, to treat them differently. So, while the government called for Jews to assimilate, at the same time they developed special policies for them which kept them separated from other groups in the country. This contradiction of calling for Jewish assimilation while enforcing Jewish separatism has continued up to the present day.

THE CIVIL WAR

The Jews first came up against Soviet discrimination during the Civil War. The Russian Civil War (1918-1920) broke out almost immediately after the Bolsheviks came to power. People who had remained loyal to the tsar attempted to overthrow the new government with the aid of certain foreign countries, such as England and France. Those who fought against the Bolsheviks were called "Whites," while the Bolshevik army was known as the "Reds." The Whites, representing the old regime in Russia, hated the Jews. Wherever the Whites were in control many Jews suffered. But neither were things very good for the Jews in the areas of Russia controlled by the Reds. The Jews who fought in the Red Army had problems with the Cossack soldiers in the ranks.

The Cossacks were a strong, individualistic group of people who had lived in the southwestern part of Russia for hundreds of years. They did not care for governmental control of any type. But because the tsar's government had done much to anger the Cossacks, the Bolsheviks were able to win many of them over to their side.

Isaac Babel, a famous Russian-Jewish writer, served with the Red Army during the Civil War, and was assigned to a unit of Cossack fighters. Babel has left a collection of stories, known as the *Red Cavalry Stories,* which discusses his experiences as an intellectual Jew among the fierce Cossacks. Below are some excerpts from these tales.

Far on in the night we reached Novograd. In the house where I was billeted I found a pregnant woman and two red-haired, scraggy-necked Jews. A third, huddled to the wall with his head covered up, was already asleep. In the room I was given I discovered turned-out wardrobes, scraps of women's fur coats on the floor, human filth, fragments of the occult crockery the Jews use only once a year, at Eastertime.

"Clear this up," I said to the woman. "What a filthy way to live!" The two Jews rose from their places and, hopping on their felt soles, cleared the mess from the floor. They skipped noiselessly, monkey-fashion, like Japs in a circus act, their necks swelling and twisting. They put down for me a feather bed ... and I lay down by the wall next to the third Jew, the one who was asleep. Faint-hearted poverty closed in over my couch...

... Lying on his back was an old man, a dead old man. His throat had been torn out and his face cleft in two; in his beard blue blood was clotted like a lump of lead.

"Good sir," said the Jewess, shaking up the feather bed, "the Poles cut his throat, and he begged them: 'Kill me in the yard so that my daughter shan't see me die.' But they did as suited them..."

(From "Crossing Into Poland")

The hatred of the Cossacks for the Jews is discussed in Babel's story, "My First Goose":

> The quartermaster, purple in the face, left us without looking back. I raised my hand to my cap and saluted the Cossacks. A lad with long straight flaxen hair and the handsome face of the . . . Cossacks went over to my little trunk and tossed it out at the gate. Then he turned his back on me and with remarkable skill emitted a series of shameful noises. . .
> . . . The sun fell upon me from behind the toothed hillocks, the Cossacks trod on my feet, the lad made fun of me untiringly. . .

This same theme of the relationship between the Cossacks and the Jews they encountered is explored in Babel's "Berestechko":

> We rode past the Cossack people . . . From behind a burial stone an old fellow with a bandore crept forth and, plucking the strings, sang to us in a childish treble of the ancient glory of the Cossacks. We listened to his songs in silence; then unfurled the standards and burst into Berestechko to the sounds of a thundering march. . .
> Notices were already posted up announcing that Divisional Commissar Vinogradov would lecture that evening on the second congress of the Comintern. Right under my window some Cossacks were trying to shoot an old silvery-bearded Jew for spying. The old man was uttering piercing screams and struggling to get away. Then Kudrya of the machine gun section took hold of his head and tucked it under his arm. The Jew stopped screaming and straddled his legs. Kudrya drew out his dagger with his right hand and carefully, without splashing himself, cut the old man's throat. Then he knocked at the closed window. . .

"Anyone who cares may come and fetch him," he said. "You're free to do so.". . .

Down below the Commissar's voice still goes on. He is passionately persuading the bewildered townsfolk and the plundered Jews.

"You are in power. Everything here is yours. No more bosses. I now proceed to the election of the Revolutionary Committee. . ."

"SOVIETIZING" THE JEW

While the Civil War was still being fought, the government set up a Commissariat of Nationalities to deal with the problems of the various national minorities in the country. The head of this new department was Joseph Stalin, who had earlier written about how the Bolsheviks would treat the Jews. One section of the new department was known as the Commissariat of Jewish Affairs, and was directed by Simeon Dimanstein. During the early 1920s the Commissariat of Jewish Affairs waged a strong campaign against organized religion in the Jewish community.

THE YEVSEKTSIIA

Even more dangerous to the Jewish community at this time was the *Yevsektsiia*, the "Jewish Section" of the Communist Party. This department was established in order to lure Jews into the Party and keep them out of other organizations. The Yevsektsiia waged a brutal campaign against the Jewish religion. Joshua Rothenberg, a noted authority on Soviet Jewry, discusses the work of the Yevsektsiia in an article

57

entitled "Jewish Religion in the Soviet Union" (printed in L. Kochan, *Jews in Soviet Russia Since 1917*).

For several hundred years, the Jews living in the territories now included in the Soviet Union had formed their own religious institutions, customs, and modes of religious observance. They enjoyed a long history of national and religious semi-autonomy, organized principally within the framework of the *Kehillah* [Jewish communal council] and its affiliated organizations. These activities and distinctive religious practices survived well past the Revolution of October 1917.

Although the tsarist regime confined the Jews to the overcrowded hamlets and towns of the Pale of Settlement, stifling their talents and energies by discrimination and exclusion from many occupations, it did not, as a rule, interfere too deeply in the inner affairs of the Jewish community. This particular situation allowed the Jewish community of tsarist Russia to make use of its own resources, and to develop, in spite of discrimination and persecution, a meaningful Jewish life and Jewish culture...

The Bolshevik Revolution of October 1917 altered the situation of Russian Jews perhaps more radically than that of other national groups in the Russian empire...

The Yevsektsiia had a double purpose: to enforce government policies on the Jewish milieu, and to "enlighten the Jewish masses in the materialistic world outlook."

In its first years of existence, the Yevsektsiia employed a peculiar form of persuasion drawn from its arsenal of anti-religious propaganda — namely, the "community trials." These trials were conducted against the Jewish religion in general, against the *cheder* [religious primary school] and *yeshiva* [religious secondary school], and against particular Jewish holidays and observances. . . .

The local authorities, with the help of the Yevsektsiia, now embarked on the forceful liquidation of the primary and secondary Jewish schools, even in those localities where public schools were not yet available for all children. . . .

In many towns, religious Jews vigorously opposed the closing of synagogues on any pretext. For instance, in Vitebsk, in 1921, worshippers openly refused to vacate a synagogue requisitioned for a children's dormitory; a large group of Jews assembled in the yard, donned prayer shawls, and refused to move. Force had to be used to take over the synagogue. Ironically, it turned out that instead of a children's dormitory, a school for adults was opened on the premises. . . .

Rothenberg goes on to explain that the most violent activities of the Yevsektsiia occurred before Passover and before the High Holidays each year. The aspect of the campaign which irritated Jews the most was the street parade, which was often used by the Yevsektsiia as a means of disrupting services inside major synagogues.

The Yevsektsiia also conducted "trials" against such practices as Sabbath observance and circumcision. As time went on, its activities became even more disgraceful. If the Whites murdered the Jews quickly, the Reds were different only in that they did so slowly.

By the mid-1920s, only seven years after the revolution, most Soviet Jews realized that the "new society" of the Bolsheviks was not what they had thought it would be. The Civil War had shown them that neither the Whites nor the Reds were friends of the Jews. The years following the fighting taught Soviet Jewry that Bolshevik policy had, in many ways, replaced the Russian Church as the major source of anti-Semitism in Russia. Instead of being known as "Christ killers," the Jews were now "class enemies" and "anti-revolutionary elements."

But more serious developments were yet to take place. The government would come up with many more methods of dealing with the "Jewish problem."

CHAPTER SIX
The "Jewish Oppositionists"

After Lenin's death in January, 1924, a struggle broke out among the powerful Bolshevik leaders seeking to take control of the government. At the time, there were several possible successors to Lenin: Trotsky, Stalin, Zinoviev and Kamenev. All of these men, except Stalin, were Jews.

For some time, the Soviet Union had what was called "collective leadership," or leadership by a group of men. Within a relatively short time, however, Stalin succeeded in eliminating his competition, and eventually took full control of the Soviet government. The other leaders, Trotsky, Zinoviev, and Kamenev, were eliminated by trials at which they were accused of a variety of "crimes against the state." In his efforts to get rid of these rivals, Stalin intentionally played upon the anti-Semitism of party members and other people in Russia.

It is important to know that many of the Jews whom Stalin attacked did not practice their religion. In fact, one writer has called them "non-Jewish Jews." But to the Russians who listened to Stalin's attacks, this made no difference. And, if Stalin could attack Trotsky, Zinoviev and Kamenev, men who did not identify with their religion, what would he say about men who proudly called themselves Jews?

Whether Stalin's victims considered themselves Jews or not, the non-Jews who opposed them held them to be just as dangerous as any religious Jew.

A VICTIM OF BOLSHEVIK ANTI-SEMITISM

Leon Trotsky was a Jewish revolutionary who had remained in the Menshevik Party until shortly before the Revolution. After joining the Bolsheviks, he quickly rose to a position of leadership, becoming the first commander of the Red Army. Looking back on the mid-1920s in Russia, Trotsky later compared those years to a period in the French Revolution known as the "Thermidor," a time when revolutionary leaders began turning against each other, in order to bolster their own power. He wrote:

At the time of the last Moscow trial I remarked in one of my statements that Stalin, in the struggle with the Opposition, exploited the anti-Semitic tendencies in the country. On this subject I received a series of letters and questions which were, by and large — there is no reason to hide the truth — very naive. "How can one accuse the Soviet Union of anti-Semitism?" "If the USSR is an anti-Semitic country, is there anything left at all?" That was the dominant note of these letters. . . .

It has not yet been forgotten, I trust, that anti-Semitism was quite widespread in Tsarist Russia among the peasants, the petty bourgeoisie of the city, the intelligentsia and the more backward strata of the working class. "Mother" Russia was renowned not only for periodic Jewish pogroms but also for the existence of a considerable number of anti-Semitic publications which, in that day, enjoyed a wide circulation. The October Revolution abolished the outlawed status against the Jews. That, however, does not at all mean that with one blow it swept out anti-Semitism. . . Legislation alone does not change people.

. . . From the day of their birth, my sons bore the name of their mother (Sedov). They never used any other name — neither at elementary school, nor at the university, nor in their later life. As for me, during the past thirty-four years I have borne the name of Trotsky. During the Soviet period no one ever called me by the name of my father (Bronstein), just as no one ever called Stalin Dzhugashvili. . . . However, after my son, Sergei Sedov, was charged with the utterly incredible accusation of plotting to poison workers, the GPU [secret police] announced in the Soviet and foreign press that the "real"(!) name of my son is not Sedov but Bronstein. If these falsifiers wished to emphasize the connection of the accused with me, they would have called him Trotsky since politically the name Bronstein means nothing at all to anyone. But they were out for other game; that is, they wished to emphasize my Jewish origin and the semi-Jewish origin of my son . . . at the time of the expulsions of the Opposition from the party, the bureaucracy purposely emphasized the names of Jewish members of casual and secondary importance. . .

After Zinoviev and Kamenev joined the Opposition the situation changed radically for the worse. At this point there opened wide a perfect chance to say to the workers that at the head of the Opposition stand three "dissatisfied Jewish intellectuals." Under the direction of Stalin, Uglanov in Moscow and Kirov in Leningrad carried through this line systematically and almost fully in the open. In order the more sharply to demonstrate to the workers the differences between the "old" course and the "new," the Jews . . . were removed from responsible party and Soviet posts. Not only in the country, but even in Moscow factories, the baiting of the Opposition back in 1926 often assumed a thoroughly obvious anti-Semitic character. . .

(from "Thermidor and Anti-Semitism," in *The Basic Writings of Trotsky*, edited by Irving Howe)

CAMPAIGN AGAINST THE "JEWISH OPPOSITION"

Trotsky also accused Stalin of using the press to wage a campaign of shameful anti-Semitism against the opposition. In his biography of Stalin he wrote:

I recall particularly a cartoon in the *Rabochnay Gazeta* [Workers' Gazette] entitled "Comrades Trotsky and Zinoviev." There were any number of such caricatures and doggerels of anti-Semitic character in the Party press. They were received with sly snickers. Stalin's attitude toward this growing anti-Semitism was one of friendly neutrality.

To the average Soviet Jew it must surely have been shocking that a man as powerful as Trotsky could be criticized by the press, tried in court on charges of "anti-revolutionary activities," and exiled. If such things could happen to the great Trotsky, what was in store for the unimportant Jewish tailor or farmer?

Many non-Jews were convinced by the campaign against the "Jewish opposition" that Jews could not be trusted in positions of importance. For many of these non-Jews, this was not a difficult idea to accept, for anti-Semitism was an old companion of the Russian people. "The Jews," many thought, "were government officials. They were far too powerful. The Jews robbed us in the small villages; now they will rob us by working in the government."

Trotsky spoke of this attitude:

> The Soviet regime, in actuality, initiated a series of new phenomena which, because of the poverty and low cultural level of the population, were capable of generating anew, and did in fact generate, anti-Semitic moods. The Jews are a typical city population. They comprise a considerable percentage of the city population in the Ukraine, in White Russia and even in Great Russia. The Soviet, more than any other regime in the world, needs a very great number of civil servants. Civil servants are recruited from the more cultured city population. Naturally the Jews occupied a disproportionately large place among the bureaucracy and particularly so in its lower and middle levels. Of course we can close our eyes to that fact and limit ourselves to vague generalities about the equality and brotherhood of all races. But an ostrich policy will not advance us a single step.
>
> The hatred of the peasants and the workers for the bureaucracy is a fundamental fact in Soviet life. . . it is impossible not to conclude that the hatred for the bureaucracy would assume an anti-Semitic color, at least in those places where the Jewish functionaries compose a significant percentage of the population and are thrown into relief against the broad background of the peasant masses.

The campaign against the "Jewish opposition" was but another way of dealing with the "Jewish problem." The Commissariat of Jewish Affairs and the Yevsektsiia tried to snuff out the identity of the Jewish masses. Stalin's attack on the opposition was an effort to build his own power by trampling on his Jewish associates. In a strange contradiction the Jewish masses were told they must assimilate, but the Jewish leaders who had assimilated were singled out for being Jews!

CHAPTER SEVEN
Biro-Bidzhan

Many Soviet Jews realized that one of their major problems was the fact that they did not have a territory of their own within the Soviet Union. They knew, also, that they were hated by many non-Jews because they were not involved to any great degree in agriculture. Most Jews were businessmen, professionals, government workers and craftsmen (tailors, jewelers, silversmiths, etc.). The Russian peasants despised them because they felt the Jews had no contact with the land.

The government also believed that Jews should be more involved in agriculture. Thus it was decided to establish a Jewish settlement in Biro-Bidzhan in eastern Siberia (see map).

President Mikhail Ivanovich Kalinin of the Soviet Union explained the purpose of establishing a Jewish territory in Biro-Bidzhan. (One must remember that the office of President in the USSR is only ceremonial. Stalin was actually in charge of the government when Kalinin was President.) Kalinin said of the project:

In spite of its indisputable progress, Soviet Jewry has suffered from one drawback. Unlike the other national minorities of the country, it lacked one definite center where it could concentrate its creative energy. . .

Kalinin then explained why Biro-Bidzhan was the best possible site for Jewish settlement:

Palestine, for instance, has the Arab problem which, as it is well known, seriously hinders the creation of a Jewish homeland there. . . Another reason for choosing Biro-Bidzhan is the fact that the country is extremely rich in natural resources. . . The chief attraction of Biro-Bidzhan . . . is the fact that the Soviet Government is willing to throw open its doors to Jewish settlers from outside the Soviet Union.

WERE THERE OTHER MOTIVATIONS?

The reasons behind the Biro-Bidzhan project have never been completely clear. Some historians have claimed that the idea originated with the Jewish organizations in Russia. But it seems that this is not so. Chimen Abramsky, an authority on Soviet Jewry, wrote an essay on the Biro-Bidzhan project, in which he explored several important points:

The leaders of . . . the Yevsektsiia realized the urgency of solving the problem of Jewish poverty. On their advice, therefore, the Soviet authorities were looking for another territory, free, or barely populated, so that the hostility of the native population would not be aroused. . .

The Biro-Bidzhan project was not the product of Jewish

initiative. It stemmed from the People's Commissariat of Agriculture, and was strongly supported by the Commissariat for Defence and the Agricultural Academy...

It seems that the Soviet Government was primarily prompted by strategic considerations: i.e. to safeguard its far-eastern frontier with Japan. The area was sparsely populated, and covered a large underdeveloped region at the confluence of the rivers Bira and Bidzhan...

The Soviet authorities, by creating a Jewish territorial unit, which was later to be transformed into a state unit, hoped to receive the moral and financial support of the Jews, mainly from America. The state would also, it was hoped, turn the attention, both of Soviet and foreign Jews, away from Zionism...

Considerable propagandist energies were devoted to popularizing Biro-Bidzhan among large sections of Soviet Jewry, and also among Jews abroad. The Jews responded by giving verbal approval, but refraining from migrating there. "The Jews raise their hands easily for Biro-Bidzhan, but not their feet," complained a correspondent of *Emes* in April 1928...

The first group of immigrants received free passage and a very little pocket money. In the first year, 1928, 600 permits were granted; of these, 450 went to representatives of families and 150 to individuals. In all, 654 people actually arrived in Biro-Bidzhan.

The number of Jews who migrated between 1928 and 1933 was as follows:

1928	1929	1930	1931	1932	1933
654	555	860	3,231	14,000	3,005

In 1929, it was planned to settle 3,000 families... or approximately 15,000 people. Actually about 1,000 people arrived and a large number left. In 1930 the number of Jews reached nearly 1,500 out of a population of 37,000, or 8 per cent....

The plan for 1933 was that 25,000 Jews should migrate; but less than one-eighth actually did so. That year more people left Biro-Bidzhan than arrived. . . .

To make the Biro-Bidzhan project more attractive to Jews, the Soviet Government, in May 1934, proclaimed the area a Jewish autonomous region. The President of the Soviet Union, Mikhail Kalinin, made an important speech on this occasion. . . "You ask," he said, "why the Jewish autonomous region was formed. The reason is that we have three million Jews, and they do not have a state system of their own, being the only nationality in the Soviet Union in this situation. The creation of such a region is the only means of a normal development for this nationality. The Jews in Moscow will have to assimilate. . . In ten years' time Biro-Bidzhan will become the most important guardian of the Jewish-national culture and those who cherish a national Jewish culture," he stated explicitly, "must link up with Biro-Bidzhan. . . "

> (From Chimen Abramsky, "The Biro-Bidzhan Project, 1927-1959," in *The Jews in Soviet Russia Since 1917,* edited by L. Kochan)

A DISAPPOINTING REALITY

To the disappointment of the Jews who travelled to the new settlement, Biro-Bidzhan was not a truly Jewish homeland. A knowledgeable Jewish observer, Joseph Schechtman, wrote in *Star in Eclipse:*

One speaker told the author: "We soon found that only the old streets of Biro-Bidzhan had Yiddish subtitles; that there was not a single Yiddish school in town . . . that the Yiddish theater had been liquidated as 'unprofitable' and no Yiddish films were shown."

This description is a far cry from the enthusiastic promises that had been made about the Biro-Bidzhan settlement by President Kalinin.

Several things about Biro-Bidzhan should be clear from this statement, from the remarks of President Kalinin, and from the analysis of Mr. Abramsky.

First, although the government claimed that the settlement would be established for the Jews, Jews had little say in the region's cultural and religious activities. Secondly, the government undoubtedly had hidden reasons, other than concern for its Jewish minority, to found the settlement. These motivations might have included getting foreign contributions and protecting the borders from the Japanese.

Third, Jewish migration to Biro-Bidzhan drastically increased in 1932 (see figures above) due to the development of Soviet collectives. As the process of collectivization, which will be discussed in chapter eight, became more intense, there was a great deal of pressure on the Jews to become farm workers and to join government collectives. Many Jews chose to migrate to Biro-Bidzhan rather than go to work on government farms. Fourth, and most important, it is possible that the government saw the Biro-Bidzhan project as one more way of dealing with the "Jewish problem." It wanted to lure the Jews far from the central regions of the Soviet Union, to separate them from the rest of Soviet society.

Government leaders, going all the way back to Stalin in 1913, claimed they wanted the Jews to assimilate with other groups. Yet President Kalinin warned that if Jews did not have a place like Biro-Bidzhan, they would vanish as a distinct group. Why did the government establish this settlement if they actually wanted the Jews to assimilate? Doesn't it seem that the government was calling for Jewish assimilation, while actually seeking to keep the Jews separate? Just as the Jews were singled out for special separatist policies in the early 1920s, they were encouraged to travel across all of Siberia to a separate colony in the 1930s.

This strange contradiction is the key to understanding other Soviet government policies toward the Jews.

CHAPTER EIGHT

The Jews in Russia's Iron Age

The years from 1929 to 1939 have been called Russia's "Iron Age." This was the time when Russia moved from economic backwardness to the position of a major industrial power.

The Soviets inherited an underdeveloped country from the tsar. Russia, at the time of the revolution, had great potential, but was not producing anywhere near what it was capable of. Soviet attempts to improve industrial and agricultural production were first hampered by the turmoil of the Civil War. It was most dificult to build up factories or farms while fighting was going on.

During the mid-1920s, the government could do little because the country was still feeling the effects of revolution, world war and civil war. Not until the end of the decade, when Stalin was in full control of the USSR, were efforts undertaken to strengthen Soviet industry and agriculture.

In the field of farming, Stalin began a program known as collectivization. Collectivization meant that small farms, which before the revolution were owned by independent farmers, were combined or "collectivized" into larger units. Each farmer gave all of his equipment, land and other supplies to the collective. All of the farmers of the collective then used the land and supplies together. Now the State owned the land, but the farmers lived on it and "managed" it. After the harvest each year, the collective gave a certain portion of its crops to the government, to be sold in the cities; the rest was used by the farmers themselves.

GROWING PAINS

At about the time that collectivization was taking place in the countryside, the Soviet Union began a rapid expansion of its industry. There were serious shortages of steel, rubber, coal and consumer goods, such as clothing, home appliances and furniture. Factory workers had to work long hours, often seven days a week, in order to increase production. Despite these problems, Russia succeeded in becoming one of the major industrial powers in the world.

Both collectivization and industrialization directly affected Soviet Jewry. Thousands of Jewish farmers fled to the cities in order to escape being forced to work on government collective farms and, despite government efforts, the percentage of Jews involved in farming steadily decreased throughout the 1930s. The children of rural families, who would otherwise have remained on farms, became city-dwellers, far removed from the countryside.

And in the cities, many Jews became involved in the development of Soviet industry. Men who had been privately employed carpenters, watchmakers, tailors and shoemakers, went to work in government-owned factories. Other Jews who were doctors, dentists, lawyers and teachers found their places in the new economic system.

Some Jews who had owned private businesses, such as food stores, clothing shops, furniture stores and the like, could not adjust so easily. These Jews found that they could no longer run their businesses; they were now "class enemies" of the State. Some attempted to find new jobs, while others moved about the country in search of food. It has been estimated that by 1930, one-third of Soviet Jewry was without any income whatever.

But the Jews were not alone in their suffering. Thousands of Soviet farmers died during those years as a result of famine. In the cities, unsanitary conditions and long working hours caused the deaths of Jews and Gentiles alike. It was a terrible time for all Soviet citizens.

STALIN'S VICTIMS

The Jews were not unique in their economic suffering, but they encountered some "special" attention in the area of Soviet religious and cultural policy. Stalin launched a strong campaign to halt the education of Jewish children in separate schools. Several hundred thousand Jewish children were forced into government schools where no religious instruction was permitted, and the enrollment in Jewish schools decreased.

All synagogues were required to get a permit from the government in order to occupy their own buildings. Rabbis lost the right to vote. Congregations had to apply for a special permit in order to hold High Holiday services; when the permit was not issued, the congregation could not use the synagogue. While a few Jews prayed in their homes in private groups, the activities of the KGB (Soviet Secret Police) made this an extremely dangerous thing to do. Most Jews prayed alone or not at all.

If Stalin's policy in the 1930s threatened Jewish religious existence, his use of the "purge" threatened the actual lives of countless Jews. A purge is a campaign of arrests, trials, imprisonments and executions, carried on by the government in order to get rid of supposed "enemies of the people." Beginning in 1936, thousands of people, Jews and Gentiles, were charged with such crimes as spying, plotting to overthrow the government, treason, and similar offenses, and sentenced to long prison terms or to death. It is difficult to determine exactly why Stalin undertook such a policy. Perhaps he wished to eliminate anyone who did not completely agree with his way of running the country. More likely, he believed he could best retain his control of the country by making the people afraid to protest government policies in any way.

THE ANTI-SEMITIC COMPONENT

The Jews were not the only ones who were "purged." Indeed there were millions of victims; members of all religious groups and nationalities were arrested and imprisoned. But because there were so many Jews in government positions and party posts, they suffered to a very great degree.

The purge trials were different from the pogroms of tsarist Russia. During the pogroms, the government made it appear that mobs were attacking Jews against the wishes of the authorities, and feeble attempts were made to punish the rioters. But now, the government itself was doing the attacking, by means of a "legal" trial. People who were accused often did not even know what the charges were. They were forced to confess to these unknown crimes, and to incriminate other people who were also "guilty" of acts against the government. Each trial led to still more trials.

Robert Conquest, in his book *The Great Terror*, comments on anti-Semitic influences in the purges:

> The anti-Semitism . . . was in accord with Stalin's general exploitation of prejudices, and of the gullibility and pliability of men in general. . .

Regarding the purge of German Communists in the late 1930s, Conquest says:

> Several of the arrested were Jews. This did not save them from charges of fascist espionage. . . An interrogator is quoted as saying, "The Jewish refugees are Hitler's agents abroad."

It should be easy to see how ridiculous these charges were. How could Jews work for Hitler's government as foreign agents? Yet the Russian people believed these charges. If Stalin said something, it was true! Conquest goes on to say that the purges virtually wiped out Soviet Zionists, and that other Zionists did nothing to help their Russian colleagues:

> Dr. Margolin [a prominent Zionist] remarks that "an entire generation of Zionists has died in Soviet prisons, camps and in exile"; and he comments that the Zionists of the outside

77

world were never able to help them, not only because of the difficulties, but because "We did not care. I do not remember seeing a single article about them in the prewar papers. Not the least effort was made to mobilize public opinion and alleviate their fate."

The "Iron Age" cost the Soviet Union literally millions of lives. Many people died on the farms and in the cities, and additional thousands of people died in Soviet prisons and work camps, where they had been sentenced for crimes they did not commit.

The Jews had more than their share of all this suffering. The small number of Jews involved in farming were forced into collective farms or fled to the cities. In the cities, where Jews were labelled "class enemies," they were forced to seek new occupations. Then the axe of the purge fell upon them. And while all this was taking place, the government carried on a constant campaign to stamp out Jewish religious life wherever it still existed.

The events of the 1920s had shown the Jews that the promise of the revolution had not been kept. The events of the 1930s taught them that the government had chosen to eliminate them as a people.

UNIT III : SOVIET JEWRY TODAY

CHAPTER NINE
Soviet Jewry and World War II

In 1939, Soviet Russia signed a treaty with Nazi Germany. According to the agreement, neither country would attack the other. The pact also included a detailed division of eastern Europe between the two powers. Russia received parts of eastern Poland, Latvia, Estonia, Lithuania, Bessarabia and several other areas. As a result of this division, approximately two million Jews were added to the three million already living under Soviet control. This gave Russia the largest Jewish population in the world.

In the summer of 1941, Hitler broke his pact with Stalin. German troops crossed into Soviet territory; Russia entered the war against Fascism. The Nazi advances into Russia effectively divided the country into two sections: Nazi-occupied, and Soviet-controlled.

For the Jews of Russia, the war brought important changes The first of them occurred before the war, so it is necessary to go back a few years.

BRINGING THE OUTSIDERS INTO LINE

When the Soviets took control of parts of eastern Europe as a result of the treaty with Germany, they found a large, fairly prosperous Jewish population. Stalin quickly realized that these shopkeepers, rabbis, intellectuals and manufacturers could not be permitted to influence the Jews who lived in the Russian sections of the Soviet Union. He therefore entrusted the Soviet secret police with the job of changing the attitudes and style of living of the new Jewish population. The Jews of eastern Europe were forced to give up their former citizenship and take an oath of loyalty to Russia. Anyone who refused, was deported to Siberia. This meant that he was forcibly taken away from his family and friends, shipped several thousand miles across Russia, and settled in the frigid wastes of Siberia. Despite this terrible punishment, several hundred thousand Jews refused to pledge their loyalty to the Soviet Union, and were sent to Siberia.

SPECIAL VICTIMS OF THE WAR

Ironically, those Jews who were deported were far luckier than their relatives and friends who remained behind in the western portions of Soviet territory. When the Germans later entered these areas, the Jews who came under their control were virtually wiped out.

Elie Wiesel, in his book *The Jews of Silence,* has made the following comment about Nazi treatment of Soviet Jewry:

... hundreds of thousands of Jews, old men, women, and children, in the Ukraine and White Russia, from Minsk to Kiev, from Lvov to Vilna. Murdered or thrown alive into mass graves, long before the ovens of Auschwitz began to cover heaven and earth with human ashes.

The evidence indicates that the vast majority of Soviet Jews in the areas controlled by the Nazis perished. Dmitri Manuilsky, the Ukrainian delegate to the San Francisco Conference of 1945 (at which the United Nations was founded), said in an interview that most of the Jews of the Ukraine were slaughtered by the Germans. In Podolia, 200,000 Jews were murdered; in Kiev, 132,000; in Odessa, most of the city's 180,000 Jews were eliminated by the Nazis.

The pattern was the same in White Russia. Nearly 160,000 Jews lived in four of the area's major cities before the war. After the Germans were driven out, only about 18,000 Jews remained.

THE TRAGEDY OF BABI YAR

By far the most infamous slaughter of Soviet Jewry at the hands of the Nazis took place at Babi Yar, just outside of Kiev. As many as 100,000 Jews were killed there at one time. Elie Wiesel wrote this about Babi Yar:

... Finally the realization comes that there is really no need for you to be shown that spot, where in the year 1941 between Rosh Hashanah and Yom Kippur who knows how many Jews were buried, dead or alive. The government guides are right; there is no reason to go there, there is

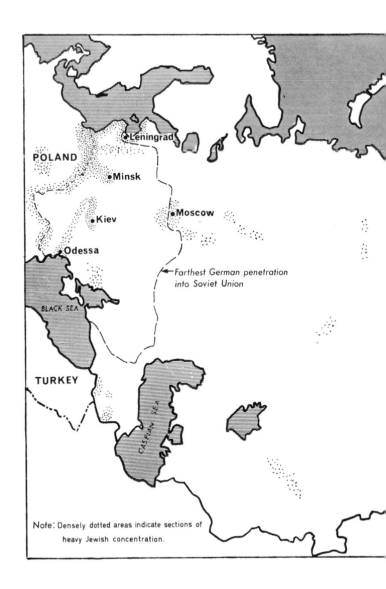

POLAND

●Leningrad

●Minsk

●Kiev

●Odessa

●Moscow

←Farthest German penetration
into Soviet Union

BLACK SEA

TURKEY

CASPIAN SEA

Note: Densely dotted areas indicate sections of
heavy Jewish concentration.

nothing to see at Babi Yar. You can see it downtown, in every square and on every street; . . .

How many Jews were killed at Babi Yar? Exact estimates are hard to come by. Some say seventy thousand, others a hundred and fifty thousand. Unlike those in Auschwitz, the Germans and their local collaborators here did not bother with statistics. . .

Eyewitnesses say that for months after the killings the ground continued to spurt geysers of blood. One was always treading on corpses. Only recently someone dug up a new mass grave, and it is generally held that this was not the last. So it is impossible to rely on figures; the dead themselves ensure the need for occasional revisions of former estimates.

Non-Jews in Kiev do not like to talk about Babi Yar. Even the quasi-official spokesmen of the Jewish community prefer to pass over it in silence rather than admit the simple, cruel, incriminating fact that the general populace of Kiev, including faithful members of the Communist Party, did not lift a finger to prevent the mass murders. . .

The terrible reality of Babi Yar cannot help but shame anyone with even the slightest bit of compassion for his fellow man. The shame comes from the recognition that men are capable of doing such a thing to other men. Feelings of grief have not been limited only to Jews. Perhaps the best-known comment has come from a non-Jewish Russian, Yevgeny Yevtushenko, author of a world-famous poem entitled "Babi Yar":

> No monument stands over Babi Yar.
> A drop sheer as a crude gravestone.
> I am afraid.
>> Today I am as old in years
> as all the Jewish people.
> Now I seem to be a Jew.

Here I plod through ancient Egypt.
Here I perish crucified, on the cross,
and to this day I bear the scars of nails.
I seem to be Dreyfus.
The Philistine
       is both informer and judge.
I am behind bars.
       Beset on every side.
Hounded,
       spat on,
            slandered.
Squealing, dainty ladies in flounced
Brussels lace
stick their parasols into my face.
I seem to be then
       a young boy in Byelostok.
Blood runs, spilling over the floors.
The bar-room rabble-rousers
give off a stench of vodka and onion.
A boot kicks me aside, helpless.
In vain I plead with these pogrom bullies.
While they jeer and shout,
       "Beat the Yids, Save Russia!"
some grain-marketeer beats up my mother.
O my Russian people!
            I know
               you
are international to the core.
But those with unclean hands
have often made a jingle of your
purest name.
I know the goodness of my land.
How vile these anti-Semites —
            without a qualm
they pompously called themselves
"The Union of the Russian People"!

I seem to be

        Anne Frank

transparent

        as a branch in April.

And I love

        And have no need of phrases.

My need

    is that we gaze into each other.

How little we can see

        or smell!

We are denied the leaves,

        we are denied the sky.

Yet we can do so much —

           tenderly

embrace each other in a dark room.

They're coming here?

    Be not afraid. Those are the booming

sounds of spring:

        spring is coming here.

Come then to me,

        Quick, give me your lips.

Are they smashing down the door?

        No, it's the ice breaking. . .

The wild grasses rustle over Babi Yar.

The trees look ominous,

        like judges.

Here all things scream silently.

        and, baring my head,

slowly I feel myself

        turning gray.

And I myself

    am one massive, soundless scream

above the thousand thousand buried here.

I am

        each old man

          here shot dead.

I am
                every child
                            here shot dead.
Nothing in me
                    shall ever forget!
The "Internationale," let it
                                thunder
when the last anti-Semite on earth
is buried forever.
In my blood there is no Jewish blood.
In their callous rage, all anti-Semites
must hate me now as a Jew.
For that reason
                I am a true Russian!

THE DECIMATION OF RUSSIAN JEWRY

Stalin always claimed that it was only his evacuation of large numbers of Jews from Nazi-occupied territories that saved them from Nazi persecution. Stalin lied, however. Only the Jews who had been deported to Siberia before the war escaped mass murder.

Before the war, Russia had a Jewish population of approximately five million (see chart below). In 1959, fourteen years after the war, the Soviet Jewish population was only about two-and-one-half million. As many as two-and-a-half million Jews perished during the Nazi occupation of the Soviet Union!

POPULATION OF JEWS IN RUSSIA
(Best possible estimates)

1820	1,600,000	(400,000 of these lived in Poland)
1851	2,400,000	(600,000 of these lived in Poland)
1880	4,000,000	(1,000,000 of these lived in Poland)
1910	5,600,000	(Polish figures unavailable)
1937	3,000,000[1]	
1939	5,000,000[2]	
1959	2,265,000[3]	

[1] The tremendous decrease from 1910 is due basically to the changes in territorial sovereignty brought about by World War I and the various international agreements that followed. Areas in eastern Europe with large Jewish populations were removed from Russian control.

[2] This increase is due to the fact that large portions of eastern Europe, areas with high concentrations of Jewish inhabitants, were acquired by the Soviets as a result of a treaty with Germany in 1939.

[3] The marked decrease is due to three basic factors: Russia's loss of parts of eastern Europe with high Jewish concentrations after World War II; the emigration of some Soviet Jews to eastern Poland and other European countries; the large scale extermination of Soviet Jews — estimated at over two million people — by the Nazis.

JEWS IN A DIVIDED USSR

The Nazi invasion had divided the USSR into two parts: Nazi-occupied and Soviet-controlled. The Jews in the Soviet-held sections knew little or nothing about what was happening to their co-religionists several hundred miles to the west. They were kept in the dark purposely by Stalin. He was only too familiar with the anti-Semitism which was widespread among the Russian people. Since Stalin needed all the help he could get for his fight against the Nazis, he did not want the Russian people to know that the Germans were persecuting Jews. This knowledge might make them more sympathetic toward the Germans. It might also make Stalin appear to be a defender of the Jews, a role which he had no desire to play.

Stalin also wanted to win as much support as possible, both within Russia and in the United States and Great Britain, for the Soviet war effort. For this purpose he established a Soviet Jewish Anti-Fascist Committee. He hoped that it would enable him to obtain large sums of foreign money to aid in the fight against the Germans. He believed, correctly, that Jews all over the world, and especially in America, would donate much money to aid Jews less fortunate than themselves and to help defeat the Nazis.

STALIN SEEKS JEWISH PROPAGANDISTS

Stalin released two former Bundists, Victor Alter (see chapter three, section on the Bund) and Henryk Erlich, from prison and asked them to draft an outline for the Jewish Anti-Fascist Committee. However their plan was not acceptable to Stalin for several reasons. It delegated too much power to the Committee. Alter and Erlich also requested that the group be permitted to carry on discussions with Jewish leaders in other countries. As far as Stalin was concerned, this idea resembled Zionism too closely. Alter and Erlich also wanted the Committee to take an active role in bringing relief to Soviet Jews displaced by the war. Stalin would not permit the organization to assume such a welfare role.

Stalin's reaction to the proposal was to order the execution of Alter and Erlich. Both were shot soon afterwards. But Stalin still needed a Jewish Anti-Fascist Committee. The original plan was then revised in accordance with Stalin's conception, and in 1942, the establishment of the JAC (as it was commonly known) was announced.

The JAC proved very successful in winning the support of Soviet and foreign Jewry for the war against Germany. In addition to its fund raising activities, the Committee published much Jewish literature, and generally became a major supporter of Jewish cultural activity in the Soviet Union. While Jews certainly suffered all of the hardships brought on by war (and far beyond that in the Nazi-occupied territories), their war-time lives within the Soviet-held sections of eastern Europe were an improvement over what they had been in the 1930s.

At one point, the chairmen of the JAC, Solomon Mikhoels and Lt. Col. Itzik Feffer, were sent to the United States to raise money for the cause. They brought back large sums of money as well as warm greetings and requests for more contacts from American Jewry.

Soviet Delegates Urge Unity Here

Prof. Michoels and Lieut. Colonel Feffer Say That Upon It Depends Allied Victory

47,000 at Polo Grounds Rally Hear Messages From Willkie and Other Leaders
Two minutes of cheering by an

audience of 47,000 persons at the Polo Grounds last night greeted speakers who called on the United States to open a second front in Europe at the earliest possible moment.

The meeting was held to welcome Prof. Solomon Michoels and Lieut. Col. Itzik Feffer, members of a Soviet delegation to the United States, and the first burst of cheers came when Newbold Morris, President of the City Council, representing the city government, pictured America as eagerly awaiting "the day, hour and minute of the second front."

Cheers came a second time when Dr. Stephen S. Wise, president of the American Jewish Congress, declared that "England and America should not delay one hour more than is necessary" in invading Europe. The two Soviet spokesmen also received ovations as they pleaded for unbreakable solidarity of the United Nations and assailed any criticism of the Soviet Union as a blow to the democratic cause.

Messages of greeting were read at the rally from Wendell L. Willkie; former Governor Herbert Lehman, director of the Office of Foreign Relief and Rehabilitation Operations; Professor Albert Einstein and many others. More than

$100,000 was pledged at the rally for a hospital in Leningrad.

The rally, held under the auspices of the Committee of Jewish Writers and Artists and of the Jewish Council of Russian War Relief, was opened with the singing of the Star Spangled Banner, the Hatikvah and the Internationale.

"The Red Army," Professor Michoels said, "avenges the bestial atrocities of the Nazi enemy. Shoulder to shoulder with all the peoples of the Soviet Union, the Jews of our country wage battle against the enemy. We are witnessing now the most righteous, yea, the holiest but also the bloodiest and most gruesome, war. The unity and brotherhood of the United Nations will decide the struggle."

Pleading for Jewish unity as an essential element of Allied unity, Colonel Feffer gave personal testimony to the reports that huge masses of Soviet, Polish, German and Rumanian Jews have been saved from Nazi extermination by the Soviet Government and enumerated individual acts of heroism on the part of Jews against the Nazi terror.

"The Jews of the Soviet Union and the United States are the majority of the Jewish people,"

Colonel Feffer said. "Together we are ten million Jews. Upon us lies the responsibility of the fate of the Jewish people. The enemy has already destroyed about four million of our people, almost a fourth. Unity is the surest guarantee of victory. He who speaks against the unity of our people aids the enemy. He who speaks against the Soviet Union acts contrary to the interests of our people."

Referring to "our great leader, Stalin," Colonel Feffer warned the audience "not to underestimate the present German offensive in Russia."

"The Nazi beast is wounded but he is not yet dead," he said. "But be sure we will strain all our powers to smash his new offensive as we smashed those that came before. We will win this war, but until we do we must not think of anything else."

... Among the speakers who addressed the rally, attended by representatives of many Jewish and non-Jewish cultural, religious, civic, fraternal and social organizations, were Sholem Asch, author; James McLeish, representing the United Radio, Electrical and Machine Workers of America, CIO; James N. Rosenberg, chairman of the Agro-Joint; Nahum Goldman, member of the Zionist World

Executive and head of the World
Jewish Congress; William Feinberg,
secretary of Local 802 of the
Musicians Union, and many others.
B. Z. Goldberg was chairman of the
rally...

(*The New York Times,* July 9, 1943)

ROOM FOR HOPE

There is an old political saying that "The public has a short memory." People do indeed quickly forget the wrongs done them. To a certain extent, this was true of the Jews in Russia. The memories of the events of the 1920s and 1930s faded away in the atmosphere created by the JAC. Of course, the tragedy of the Jews in the Nazi-occupied regions could not be forgotten, but in a strange way it served to improve the attitude of Soviet Jews toward the Russian government. The Jews could not help but compare the massacres carried out by the Nazis to the considerably better conditions in the Soviet-held areas.

Soviet Jews who survived the war felt that there might be some room for optimism regarding the future. Perhaps the terrible experience of war would unite the Soviet people behind the idea that all people deserved equality of treatment. Perhaps Stalin would remember the service which the Jews of the JAC performed in helping the Soviet war effort.

CHAPTER TEN
Stalin and the Jews

Solomon Mikhoels had long been a loyal follower of the Bolshevik regime, but he had never given up his attachment to Jewish tradition and customs. Over the years, he had become one of the most famous actors of the Russian Yiddish stage. Thus, when the time came to choose prominent Soviet Jews to direct the JAC, Stalin had named Mikhoels as the committee's chairman.

A TOOL OF NATIONAL POLICY

As long as the war continued, Stalin needed the JAC and the world-wide support which Mikhoels could arouse for the Soviet war effort. However, when the war ended, the JAC was no longer necessary. Perhaps not realizing Stalin's true feelings toward the JAC, Mikhoels embarked on a post-war campaign of aiding Jews left homeless and hungry by the war. Then, in January 1948, Mikhoels was murdered in Minsk. The government publicly deplored the incident, but fourteen years later a

Lithuanian Communist newspaper admitted that the murder had been carried out by Stalin's secret police.

Mikhoels' death was followed by the arrest and execution of many of the JAC leadership, including some of the most prominent figures in the Soviet Jewish community. The method chosen to eliminate them became known as the "Crimean Affair."

Toward the end of the war, the JAC had taken up the question of what to do with the homeless Jewish refugees throughout Russia. Many plans were considered, but it was finally decided to support the settlement of these Jews in a semi-autonomous region in the Crimea. When Stalin heard the proposal, his reaction was to reject it as unsatisfactory. No further comments were made at that time.

However, several years after the war, many of the committee's members were suddenly charged with being involved in a conspiracy to detach the Crimea from the Soviet Union. It was claimed that they were working with foreign agents in an effort to undermine the Soviet Union from within. Their "crime" was punished by their deaths.

THE "PRAGUE TRIALS"

But this was only a small part of what would befall the Jews of Russia in the years after the war. Toward the end of 1952, a public trial began in Prague, Czechoslovakia. Like other countries in eastern Europe whose political and social activities were controlled by the USSR after World War II, Czechoslovakia appeared to remain independent, but its political system became Communist. Russia dictated what the Czechoslovak "satellite" government could or could not do.

The Prague trial was held to prosecute Rudolf Slansky, Secretary-General of the Czechoslovak Communist Party, and a Jew. Slansky was accused of working with American agents and world Zionist figures against the interests of the Soviet Union. As the trial progressed, more and more people were accused of similar crimes. Nearly all of these people were Jews.

The following accounts of the trials are excerpts of Russian press reports:

As previously reported, at the afternoon session of November 20 the court began to cross-examine the defendants. The first to be cross-examined was Rudolf Slansky, leader of the anti-state conspiratorial center. The defendant pleaded guilty to espionage, high treason, sabotage and military treason. Slansky testified that he "organized the anti-state center and headed it for many years." He stated: "This center where we concentrated many diverse capitalist elements, many of which became agents of the imperialist intelligence services, the French and primarily the American intelligence services, engaged in hostile activities in the interests and in the service of the American and British imperialists. These activities were directed toward liquidating the people's democratic system and toward restoring capitalism. . ."

Slansky testified that he was also connected with Zionist organizations, the instrument of American imperialism. The conspirators were also connected with Masonic organizations and relied on them in their subversive activities. . .

The witness Goldstuckers, former Czechoslovak Ambassador to Israel and member of the conspiratorial center, testified that on missions he engaged in espionage for Slansky and Geminder and gave espionage information to the British agent Zilliacus. The witness confirmed that Slansky was directly connected with Zilliacus through the accused Arthur London. The accused Geminder and Frejka were also connected with Zilliacus. While in Prague Gold-stuckers helped Slansky to establish contact with the Czechoslovak people's enemies among the Zionists, agents of the imperialist intelligence services. . .

Josef Frank [a Jew], a former Deputy General Secretary of the Czechoslovak Communist Party Central Committee, appeared before the court. Finding himself in 1939 in the German death camp Buchenwald, he quickly gained the Hitlerites' confidence, beat up Russian and French prisoners-of-war and drew up lists of prisoners whom the fascists then shot. Frank was included in the list of war criminals and was liable for trial by a military tribunal, but he managed to hide and became one of Slansky's closest assistants. . .

> (*Pravda*, November 22, 1952; reprinted in
> *The Current Digest of the Soviet Press*, January 3, 1953)

The above excerpt from the Soviet press indicates how figures were implicated in the original accusations against Slansky. By associating Secretary-General Slansky with a "conspiratorial center," the Soviets could bring in other people and condemn them as well. Thus, prominent Czechoslovak Jewish Communists, such as Geminder, Frejka and Frank, were also charged with crimes against the state and sentenced to death for treason.

THE "DOCTORS' PLOT"

But still more was to come! Early in 1953, as reports of the so-called "Prague Trials" began to subside, a new scandal was disclosed. A group of doctors working in the Kremlin, nearly

STALIN AND THE JEWS

all of whom were Jews, were accused of carrying out a plot to murder high officials in the Soviet government and military. They were said to be agents of "American Zionists," working for the overthrow of the Soviet government.

Agencies of state security of the Soviet Union have discovered a group of wrecker doctors who, concealed by the lofty calling of doctor, trampled on the sacred banner of honor. Their aim was to cut short the lives of active personalities of the Soviet Union by means of wrecker medical treatment. In this manner these highway murderers killed leading personages of the Soviet state, A.A. Zhdanov and A.S. Scherbakov. Their foremost intention was to undermine the health of Soviet leading military cadres in order to weaken the defense of the Soviet Union. . .

It has been established that the hand of American and British imperialists and their agents directed the sabotage activity of this group of murdering doctors. The criminals sold themselves and served American and British intelligence services. The wrecker doctors were closely connected with the international Jewish bourgeois nationalist organization which bears the name "Joint," which was set up by American intelligence agencies supposedly for material aid to Jews in other countries; in reality this organization has conducted and is now conducting, under the supervision of the American intelligence service, extensive espionage, terrorist and subversive activity in a number of countries, including the Soviet Union. . .

Besides the "Joint" organization, other espionage and subversive organizations, set up by the American and British imperialists, worked in Transcarpathia. "Jewish Colonization Association" was one example. "Jewish National Fund," "Poale Zion," etc., were others. . . Such an organization as "League for the Working People of Palestine," which was headed by the well-known director of the Jewish Gymnasium in Mukachev, Chaim Kugel, was a recruitment center for agents and saboteurs. In addition, other organizations and groups of Zionists, such as "Mizrachi," "Viso" and "Bytari" were set up by American dollars.

(Pravda Ukrainy, February 13, 1953; reprinted in *The Current Digest of the Soviet Press,* March 14, 1953)

The campaign against the Jews gained momentum. "Scandals" were uncovered by the Soviet press, which depicted Jews all over the country as cheaters, liars, and even saboteurs. Prominent Jewish writers, men whose brilliance had been acknowledged by Jews and Gentiles throughout the world, were first stopped from publishing, and then imprisoned for ridiculous reasons. Some, such as Lozovsky, Bergelson, Feffer and Markish, were executed on charges of treason. Stalin's obsession even extended to a plan for massive deportation of Jews from the Ukraine and other portions of western Russia to eastern Siberia. Fortunately, he never lived to carry such a plan into action.

A CHANGE OF HEART

While these events were taking place in the Soviet Union, relations with Israel were changing drastically. In the first years following the end of the war, Russia had supported the establishment of an independent Jewish state in the Middle East. Although it is difficult to determine Stalin's reasons, it is most likely that he saw the existence of such a state to be a way of weakening British power in the Mediterranean region. Great Britain had been in control of the Palestine area for many years and the Soviets wished to push the British out of the Middle East. Russia voted in the United Nations in favor of the formation of a Jewish state, and then granted recognition to Israel.

When Golda Meir, the first Israeli Ambassador to the Soviet Union, came to Moscow, massive demonstrations took place. Soviet Jewry extended a most enthusiastic welcome to Mrs. Meir. Apparently, Stalin considered the welcome too enthusiastic. The demonstrations were ordered stopped, and many of those who participated were arrested.

The early 1950s saw a worsening in relations between Russia and Israel. The final break came in February 1953, with a report that the Soviet Legation in Israel had been bombed. The Soviet press account of the incident accused the Israeli officials of working with the terrorists who carried out the bombing.

A terrorist act directed against the Soviet Legation in Israel was carried out by malefactors February 9 with the obvious connivance of the police. At 2235 hours on that day a bomb was exploded by criminals on the premises of the U.S.S.R. Legation, as a result of which K.V. Yershova, wife of the Minister; A.P. Sysoyeva, wife of a Legation official; and I.G. Grishin, an official of the Legation were injured. Part of the Legation building was destroyed.

It should be noted that this vile crime was preceded by an unbridled slanderous campaign against the Soviet Union with the participation of Israeli officials, who openly incited to hostile actions against the Soviet Union and the U.S.S.R. Legation in Israel.

On February 10 the President and the Ministry of Foreign Affairs of Israel sent notes to the Soviet Legation in which they declared their apologies for this act on behalf of the government of Israel.

These statements and apologies by the government of Israel are, however, in complete contradiction with the numerous facts of direct participation of representatives of the government of Israel in the kindling of hatred of the Soviet Union and incitement to hostile acts against the U.S.S.R. . . . .

(*Pravda,* February 12, 1953; reprinted in
The Current Digest of the Soviet Press, March 14, 1953)

AN ANSWER TO THE PUZZLE?

Why had all of these events taken place? It was true that the Yevsektsiia had carried on an anti-Semitic campaign in the 1920s; that the "Jewish Opposition" had been the victims of anti-Semitism; that thousands of Jews had suffered as a result of the policies of the "Iron Age." But why did Stalin undertake such a brutal effort against the Jews between 1948 and 1953 (the year of his death)?

The answer to this question can never really be known. Stalin never told anyone. We can only guess at his reasons. Certainly one motive for these actions was Stalin's personal anti-Semitism. From his early years as a student of the Russian clergy, Stalin had been exposed to feelings of hatred for the Jew. His essay, "Marxism and the National Question," clearly condemned the desire of many Jews to preserve their religion and culture. And he did not hesitate to use anti-Semitism as a weapon in his struggles with political rivals.

But why did these massive persecutions come precisely when they did, and not at some other time? The explanation of this lies in conditions within Russia before 1948. During the 1920s and 1930s, the Soviet Union was faced with far too many economic problems to devote a large effort to "dealing with the Jews." Although there were elements of anti-Semitism in the purges of the 1930s, if Stalin had limited the persecutions to the Jews, he would not have succeeded in making all Soviet citizens fear his power.

After World War II, Russia's foremost enemy became the United States. The period known as the "Cold War" began. The West (United States, England, France and other Western countries) and the East (Russia, the "satellite countries" of Eastern Europe, and China) battled for the control of neutral countries all over the world. The "fighting" was usually only with words and ideas, but it was nevertheless a dangerous combat.

It was fairly easy for Stalin to label Soviet Jewry as a negative element of society against which he could unite the rest of the Soviet people, a unity which would be necessary for the coming struggle against the Western powers. He could point to Soviet Jewry's Zionist activities, which often involved contacts with American organizations, as proof of their subversive interests. Furthermore, if Stalin could make the Soviet people believe that Israel was an enemy, he could convince them that the Soviet Jews had deep sympathies for the enemies of Russia.

The existence of the JAC and the extension of other freedoms, such as freer travel, easier communication with Jews inside Russia and abroad, and less censorship of books, caused many Soviet Jews to believe, for a short while, that there might be hope for a bright future within the Soviet Union. The events of the so-called "Black Years" convinced them that they had been wrong.

CHAPTER ELEVEN
Soviet Jewry Under Khrushchev

Joseph Stalin died in 1953. After a brief period of struggle within the Communist Party, Nikita Khrushchev emerged as Stalin's successor. Khrushchev introduced an era of "de-Stalinization," during which the brutal methods of Stalin were supposedly reversed.

For Soviet Jewry, this new era meant an end to the mass arrests, the threatening articles in the press, and the talk of worldwide Jewish conspiracies. But the damage already done to Jewish cultural and religious institutions — the shutting of synagogues, the closing of Yiddish newspapers and theaters, and the prohibition of Hebrew teaching — was not reversed.

> ... condemned to the status of an un-people, [the Jews] had been marked out for cultural extinction and their institutions had been destroyed. However, it would seem that in Khrushchev's view, this particular action of Stalin

did not fall into the category of "monstrous acts" and "rude violations of the basic Leninist principles of the nationality policy of the Soviet state"; it was a deed of prudent statesmanship. In the course of an interview with a Canadian Communist delegation, Khrushchev, in one of the unguarded moments of candor to which he is so often given, showed himself to share Stalin's view of the Jews as inherent security risks. "Khrushchev," relates the Canadian Communist Salsber (*The New Leader,* September 14, 1959), "agreed with Stalin that the Crimea, which had been depopulated at the war's end, should not be turned into a Jewish colonization center, because in case of war it would be turned into a base for attacking the U.S.S.R. . . . "

Stalin's heirs are determined not to revoke the edict against the cultural life of the Jews. The pleadings of a British Communist group that Yiddish schools and the theatre be restored, were met by Suslov with. . . "No, these things will not be reinstituted."

> (From Erich Goldhagen, "Communism and Anti-Semitism,"
> in Abraham Brumberg (ed.), *Russia Under Khrushchev*)

THE MORE IT CHANGES,
THE MORE IT REMAINS THE SAME

Khrushchev had given up the brutal tactics of the Stalinist years, but he had not abandoned the basic attitudes toward the Jews that had existed in Russia for a thousand years. He was a product of the anti-Semitic Ukrainian peasantry and of the Russian Christian Church, and he brought their prejudices with him to the "new society" of Soviet Russia.

Jewish Communists all over the world soon realized that Khrushchev's policies actually differed very little from those of Stalin when it came to the Jews. He called for Jewish assimilation, just as other Soviet leaders had done for fifty years before him, but separate Jewish passports continued to be issued and university quotas were maintained. The same old contradiction was there. Jews were criticized for not "melting" into Soviet society, but at the same time they were kept apart by a determined official policy of discrimination.

> Disillusioned and embittered, Jewish Communists in Canada, the United States, and Britain have deserted their Parties in large numbers. For many years, they had nourished a vision of Soviet Russia that bore little resemblance to reality. Their imagination had seen a land in which a multinational brotherhood, informed by love, was laboring toward the realization of Utopia under the guidance of dedicated leaders. . .
>
> . . . According to Salsberg, "Khrushchev repeated the view . . . that the majority of Soviet Jews have become integrated into the country's general life. He emphasized that such integration is historically progressive, whereas the maintenance of a separate group existence is reactionary.". . .

> (From Erich Goldhagen, "Communism and Anti-Semitism.")

In appearance Khrushchev was very much like the average Russian peasant, and he cultivated the image of a kind man. In reality, however, he was quite ruthless. Many Jewish party officials in the Ukraine were purged as Khrushchev rose to a position of power. He had done little to help the Jews during his career, despite his declarations that he favored freedom for all and even supported the right of dissatisfied citizens to try other forms of government.

Khrushchev once said:

> Now ... we've got to stop looking for a defector in every-one. We've got to stop designing our border policy for the sake of keeping the dregs and scum inside our country. We must start thinking about the people who don't deserve to be called scum — people who might undergo a temporary vacillation in their own convictions, or who might want to try out the capitalist hell, some aspects of which may still appear attractive to our less stable elements. We can't keep fencing these people in. We've got to give them a chance to find out for themselves what the world is like...

Yet, despite this apparent liberalism, Khrushchev was quite intolerant of Soviet Jewry. The editor of his memoirs has said of him:

> One of the most interesting aspects of this narrative is the way in which Khrushchev goes out of his way to condemn anti-Semitism. Guilt feelings must play their part here. There is no evidence to indicate that Khrushchev himself was ever committed actively to anti-Semitism, but time and time again he is on record as making disparaging remarks about Jews and insisting that they should be kept in their place. He may have been horrified by the pogroms of his childhood, but he did not like Jews, and as master of the Ukraine, he kept silent about the mass-murdering carried out by the Nazis (including the massacre at Babi Yar on the outskirts of Kiev). In accordance with Stalin's policy, which he later made his own, he refused to admit that Jews had suffered more than non-Jews on Soviet territory; he must also have connived at Stalin's own postwar deportation of Jews from the Ukraine into deep Siberia...

(from *Khrushchev Remembers* [memoirs])

FINAL REALIZATION

Many Jews outside of the Soviet Union still believed in the 1930s and 1940s that the revolution had not broken its promise to the Jews, that a better life was in store for Soviet Jewry than they had ever enjoyed before on Russian soil. While the events of the "Black Years" convinced many observers that Russia would never treat its Jews fairly, others interpreted the "Black Years" as the excesses of one man. They believed that Stalin had distorted the faults of the Soviet system, but that the system itself was still good.

After the death of Stalin, however, it became apparent that a system which could permit such distortions to take place was itself wrong. Individual leaders might use different tactics, but the fact remained that the Soviet experience in general had been a near fatal one for the Jews.

. . .if we survey history and compare the lofty aims, in the name of which revolutions were started, and the sorry end to which they came, we see again and again how a polluted civilization pollutes its own revolutionary offspring. . .

The necessary lie, the necessary slander; the necessary intimidation of the masses to preserve them from short-sighted errors; the necessary liquidation of oppositional groups and hostile classes; the necessary sacrifice of a whole generation in the interest of the next — it may all sound monstrous and yet it was so easy to accept while rolling along the single track of faith. . .

(From Arthur Koestler's essay in *The God That Failed,*
Richard Crossman [ed.])

THE SOVIET GOVERNMENT'S EFFORTS TO DEAL WITH THE "JEWISH PROBLEM"

Government Policy	Reaction of Jews	Government's Response
Yevsektsiia	Few joined. Most continued to observe customs despite anti-religious campaign.	Yevsektsiia disbanded in late 1920s.
War against "Opposition."	Victims executed or exiled. Most Jews can do little, because victims labelled "enemies of state."	Stalin's power increased.
Biro-Bidzhan	Little Jewish migration.	Project neglected by government and slowly dies.
Anti-Religious Program (1930s)	Many Jews stop attending religious services, sending children for religious instruction; Yiddish publications all but cease.	Program continues until World War II.
Purges (late 1930s)	Most victims do not have chance to speak out. Others fear for their own safety and remain silent.	Purge lasts until shortly before World War II. Thousands perish.
Jewish Anti-Fascist Committee	Participation.	Disbanded after war. Many leaders arrested on false charges.

112

SOVIET JEWRY UNDER KHRUSHCHEV

Crimean Affair (late 1940s – early 1950s)	Victims quickly silenced. Others can do little to challenge power of Stalin.	Strength of anti-Jewish campaign increased.
Prague Trials (Czechoslovakia, 1952)	Victims forced to admit to involvement in worldwide Zionist conspiracy. Others are shocked, but can do nothing.	Anti-Jewish campaign further strengthened.
Doctors' Plot	Again, the victims are silenced. Other Jews are unable to say or do anything in support of doctors.	Broad claims of international plot to destroy the Soviet state. Active propaganda campaign against Jews.
Israel Policy	Enthusiasm over initial Soviet support; despair at change to opposition role.	Increased hostility to Israel; better relations with Arab states.
Refusal to restore freedoms taken away in 1920s and 1930s; Refusal to permit emigration from USSR (post-Stalin).	Growing activism; underground movement.	Continuation of policy; Denial of any truth to Jewish claims of problems in USSR.

113

UNIT IV : THE FUTURE

CHAPTER TWELVE
What Will Happen?

The historical experience of Soviet Jewry can be roughly divided into three periods: Hope, Despair, Action. At first Soviet Jewry believed that the revolution would truly do away with the injustices of pre-revolutionary Russia. The tsar was gone and it was hoped that the pogroms and discriminatory laws of his era had disappeared with him. Such feelings of hope, in the case of most Soviet Jews, survived the anti-Semitism of the 1920s, even the chaos and purges of the 1930s. During the Second World War, Soviet Jews felt that the period of misunderstanding had ended; that a new era of freedom had dawned. But the "Black Years" showed them that the war period had not been an end to the darkness, but rather a mere break in the roof of the tunnel of darkness to which they saw no end. Russian Jews came to realize that the official anti-Semitism of the Soviet regime was not a series of unfortunate, misdirected events. It became clear that the Jews had always been the intended targets of a near-constant campaign of destruction and persecution. Thirty years of

Soviet rule had led to charges of worldwide Jewish conspiracies and secret plots to overthrow the government.

As leading Jewish writers, actors, doctors, teachers and party figures perished, hope was replaced with despair. Elie Wiesel's description of the eyes of Soviet Jews, written in the mid-1960s, reflects this sense of hopelessness.

> Their eyes — I must tell you about their eyes. I must begin with that, for their eyes precede all else, and everything is comprehended within them. The rest can wait. It will only confirm what you already know. But their eyes — their eyes flame with a kind of irreducible truth, which burns and is not consumed. Shamed into silence before them, you can only bow your head and accept the judgment. Your only wish now is to see the world as they do. A grown man, a man of wisdom and experience, you are suddenly impotent and terribly impoverished. Those eyes remind you of your childhood, your orphan state, cause you to lose all faith in the power of language. Those eyes negate the value of words; they dispose of the need for speech.

(from *The Jews of Silence*)

A FOCUS FOR ACTIVISM

But gradually, more like the rising of the sun than the abrupt crack of a gunshot, despair has turned to action. Soviet Jewry has come to understand the meaning of "If I am not for myself, who will be for me." It is almost as if the Jews of Russia realized and accepted the truth of what Russian Zionists had said sixty years earlier, before the revolution: The only future for Russian Jewry lies outside of Russia.

The focus of this new activism on the part of Soviet Jewry is their right to religious freedom. It might seem strange, after reading the Constitutions of the United States and of the Soviet Union, that religious freedom should be a point of difference between the two nations.

The Constitution of the United States: First Amendment	*The Constitution of the Soviet Union: Article 124*
Congress shall make no law respecting an establishment of religion, or prohibiting the free exercise thereof; or abridging the freedom of speech, or of the press; or the right of the people peaceably to assemble, and to petition the Government for a redress of grievances.	In order to ensure to citizens freedom of conscience, the church in the U.S.S.R. is separated from the state, and the school from the church. Freedom of religious worship and freedom of anti-religious propaganda is recognized for all citizens.

Despite these fine phrases, the social fabric of the Russian people made it difficult for the Jews to enjoy the guarantees of the Constitution of the Soviet Union. A comparison with the United States makes this clear.

The United States has had no history of affiliation of specific national or religious groups with particular sections of the country. There is no "Italian state," or an "Irish state" within the United States. Russia, however, developed as an empire made up of specific nationalities, each living within its traditional "homeland." The Jews were the exception to this general rule. They had always been limited to certain areas where they could live; they had always been unwelcome residents in the territory of some other national group.

In addition, Russia had a long tradition of anti-Semitism, strengthened by the teachings of the Church and the policy of the tsars. As Trotsky stated, "Changing the laws doesn't mean changing the people." The revolution did not wipe out hundreds of years of anti-Semitic tradition, even assuming that this had been a basic concern of the revolutionary leaders.

If the principal obstacle to securing equality for the Jews under Soviet control was their refusal to assimilate, we must ask, "Why did they not assimilate?" The answer to this question is that, despite what the Soviet government has said about the desirability of Jewish assimilation, it has never really wanted it to come about. Why would the Soviet government continue to enforce quotas, limiting the entry of young Jews into the major universities of the country? Why else would the Soviet government never permit the Jews to live without the disparaging label "Zhid" (Jew)? Just like the Church before it, the Soviet government continued to identify the Jew as a Jew, and single him out for "special treatment."

If this was to be the plight of Soviet Jewry, why not take the course of activism? The hope of the '20s, '30s and '40s proved to be false; the despair of the '50s and '60s was wasteful; perhaps the action of the last several years is the only answer.

LET OUR PEOPLE GO!

It is clear from what we can learn about the activities of Soviet Jewry today that they have indeed chosen the course of action. The Soviet government can no longer hide the protests of Russian Jews. They are being heard above the din of official propaganda and public denials that a new Jewish "Opposition" exists.

Soviet Union:
Nyet Is No Answer

Joseph Kazakov is a 49-year-old non-person. For ever since he asked permission to emigrate to Israel, Kazakov has brought down upon himself the full weight of official ostracism – a common punishment for Soviet Jews who, by the tens of thousands, have had the temerity to apply for exit visas that are rarely granted. But unlike the more complacent souls who populate the Soviet Union, Kazakov has refused to take *nyet* for an answer. Instead, he and 38 other Soviet Jews last week took an astonishingly bold step: they addressed an open letter to the Soviet Foreign Ministry and then passed it on to Western correspondents in Moscow. "We are ready," the Jews proclaimed, "to make our way to the state of Israel, even on foot."

To the rulers in the Kremlin, a request to leave the Soviet Union is an open admission of disloyalty. Accordingly, when the plea from the 39 Jews was beamed back to Russia by the Voice of America, Moscow responded angrily by branding them as "social outcasts." What cut Soviet propagandists to the quick was that the letter, along with similar petitions from 27 Jews in Riga and 21 from Leningrad, belied official claims that the Soviet Union's 3 million Jewish citizens feel no spiritual affinity for Israel and fully support Moscow's pro-Arab policies.

For weeks, Soviet Jews have been pressured into writing letters to newspapers against Israel and into supporting anti-Israeli resolutions at televised public meetings. The high point of this strident campaign was reached earlier this month when 31 Jews – all of them prominent in public life, the professions and the arts – were paraded before foreign correspondents in Moscow's garish Hall of Friendship. In the course of the orchestrated proceedings, an assortment of generals, writers, scientists and philosophers – and even a former woman bomber pilot – joined Deputy Premier Veniamin Dymshits (the highest-ranking Jew in the government) in rejecting "Zionist nonsense."

The evidence that the Jews had damned Israel only after considerable official prodding was unmistakable. Maya Plisetskaya, Russia's prima ballerina, stayed away from the meeting, although she could not keep her name from a statement made by the group. One Jew who did show up later told a Westerner that he had been ordered to either attend or forget about any trip abroad that he might be planning.

Before the meeting was over, it was evident that what had begun as a propaganda campaign against Israel was aimed at Jews at home as well. For underlying the Kremlin's efforts to reassure the Arabs was a warning to Jews not to criticize Moscow's policies. There was also the possibility that if they took Israel's side, Soviet Jews might find themselves cast as the scapegoats for widespread economic difficulties now plaguing the Soviet Union.

Still, the very eminence of the people gathered in the Hall of Friendship was proof that being a Jew is of itself no bar to success — at least outside of politics. Indeed, one explanation for official refusals to allow Jews to emigrate is that the Soviet Union cannot afford a brain drain. And by showing off their "good" Jews, it was clear that the Soviet leaders wanted to demonstrate that, although they are anti-Zionists, they are not anti-Semites — and thereby discourage Jews from applying to leave the country.

(*Newsweek,* March 23, 1970)

The Jews of Russia are no longer a people of silence. Nor are they a people of inaction. They have adopted the tactics of many of the "underground" movements operating in the world today. For example, a group of Jews and non-Jews attempted to hijack a Soviet airplane from Russia's Smolny Airport in June,

1970. At the trial of the so-called "Leningrad Eleven," the defendants received harsh sentences.

Soviet Union:
The Leningrad Eleven

At Leningrad's Smolny Airport last June, twelve Soviet citizens – ten of them Jews – were arrested as they walked across the tarmac toward a small airliner. The charge: planning to hijack the plane. Amid almost total secrecy, eleven of the prisoners went on trial two weeks ago in Leningrad, where they reportedly confessed that they had intended to fly the airliner to Sweden – and that the Jews among them hoped eventually to make their way to Israel. Last week, the court handed out the world's harshest punishment yet in a case of hijacking – much less an attempted hijacking. Nine of the defendants were sentenced to prison terms ranging from four to fifteen years, and the other two – Mark Dymshits, 43, and Eduard Kuznetsov, 30, both Jews – were condemned to die in front of a firing squad.

The astonishing severity of the sentences provoked an anguished outcry from both Jews and gentiles around the world. The Israeli Parliament formally called on the Kremlin to release all eleven prisoners, and a Tel Aviv newspaper claimed that the defendants had been lured into the plot by a Soviet police agent. The French Communist Party newspaper *L'Humanité* declared that "the verdict appeared to be out of proportion with the facts." In the United States, Jewish organizations and the World Council of Churches joined in the appeals for mercy, and a group of militant Jewish students carrying portraits of the Leningrad Eleven picketed the Soviet mission to the United Nations.

Under Soviet law, the sentences were technically proper, for fleeing the country is an act of treason — and merely plotting a crime is considered tantamount to actually committing it. But the Kremlin's motives appeared to go far beyond mere legalisms. Ever since the Middle East war of 1967, the 3 million Jews in the Soviet Union have taken increasing pride in their ethnic identity, and thousands of them have applied — with only rare success — for permission to leave the country. At the same time, Jews outside the Soviet Union have begun to speak out on the problems of Soviet Jewry, in the hope that they could force Moscow to allow more Jews to emigrate.

That plan seems to have backfired, for the Kremlin's stance has only hardened. Not long after the incident, at Smolny Airport, another twenty Jews were rounded up on charges of anti-Soviet

> agitation. Nine of them are
> expected to go on trial this week,
> and a court-martial is also planned
> for the twelfth member of the
> original group. Moreover, one
> Soviet newspaper charged last
> week that "Zionist circles" in the
> state of Israel had been in on the
> hijack plot, which suggested to
> some analysts that the Kremlin was
> stepping up its campaign against
> the Jews. As for the Leningrad
> Eleven, they had seven days in
> which to appeal their sentences,
> and Dymshits and Kuznetsov had
> the further option of petitioning
> the government for clemency.

(*Newsweek*, January 4, 1971)

JOINING THE STRUGGLE

American Jews have also begun to take up the fight of Soviet
Jewry. The Student Struggle for Soviet Jewry is one of the
major American groups involved in the campaign to free the
Jews of Russia.

> How long must we plead
> For the bound to be freed
> From the chains that oppress and degrade?
> How long? How long? How long?
> How long must we wait
> While the hour grows late
> And our brothers grow faint and afraid?
> Too long! Too long! Too long!

126

The concern reflected in this topical ballad is the motivating force behind a small but growing movement of youth dedicated to a Herculean task — the rescue of Soviet Jewry from cultural and religious extinction.

Over the past two academic calendar years hardly a month has passed without some student protest about the deprivations of Soviet Jewry. Rallies, vigils, marches, fasts, and prayer sessions have dotted campuses across the country. New York City in particular has been the scene of major activity. . .

These demonstrations are not haphazardly arranged. They are timed to coincide with significant Jewish or Russian events so as to most effectively arouse public opinion. . .

Like protest movements involving other political and social causes, the student effort to rescue Soviet Jewry has given birth to songs. "There's a Fire Burning" is among them:

> There's a fire burning brightly in the sky
> And the roar of thunder crashing from on high,
> I see a nation there awakening
> Iron yokes will soon be breaking,
> And a nation long oppressed shall arise —
> A nation long oppressed shall arise. . .
> A trumpet rings through the night,
> The dawn appears — we see the light,
> We wake the world, we make them see
> That our people must be free.
> Freedom's train is racing swiftly through the land
> And the tide of love is pounding on the sand,
> I can hear the whole world crying
> For a nation that's been dying,
> It will soon hold out its helping hand.

(From "Student Struggle for Soviet Jewry," by Ronald Rubin)

SSSJ's policy of mass demonstrations has four basic aims:

1. To cause the Soviet Government concern about its image due to its treatment of Jews.
2. To convince the White House that the situation of Soviet Jewry is a matter of burning concern to a very large segment of American citizenry.
3. To give much needed encouragement to Soviet Jews.
4. To arouse among Jews a new spirit of concern for the welfare and destiny of the suffering segments of world Jewry.

But American activities in support of Soviet Jewry have sometimes been more violent. For example, the Jewish Defense League (JDL) has undertaken acts of violence against Soviet officials and the offices of Soviet agencies in the United States. News accounts of mysterious bombings of Soviet facilities in New York include reports of phone messages of "Never Again!" which often follow these incidents.

One may question whether acts of destruction against Soviet facilities in the United States will convince the government in Moscow that Jews should be permitted to leave the Soviet Union. Only the final result will tell which tactic was most successful in accomplishing the goal of freeing Soviet Jewry. One thing is clear: at the present time, exit from the Soviet Union, for those Jews who are fortunate enough to achieve it, is anything but free.

THE EXIT TAX

The following table shows the average monthly income of a professional in the U.S.S.R.

Profession	*Income per month (Rubles)*
Doctor	85–150
Teacher	85–110
Research Scientist	250
Engineer	120–175
Associate Professor	200
Full Professor (PhD)	1000

In 1972, a Soviet law was passed which required that Soviet citizens given permission to leave the country must first pay the state for the education which they received. The more education received, the higher the "tax." Many Soviet Jews are highly educated and would therefore have to pay huge sums before they could leave. A comparison of the table below and the income chart above, is very instructive.

Degree	*Tax in Rubles*	*Tax in Dollars*
High School	5,400	6,750
Business Degree	3,600	4,500
Teaching Degree	4,500	5,600
Bachelor's Degree (BA)	5,500	6,775
Technical Degree	7,700	9,625
Medical Degree (MD)	8,400	10,500
Applied Arts (AA)	9,000	11,250
Art and Music Degree	9,600	12,000
Soviet PhD	12,000	15,250
University Degree	11,000	13,750
Institute of Science	17,600	22,000
Professor	19,000	23,750

(Both tables are from "Keeping Posted," December 1972, a publication of the Union of American Hebrew Congregations)

Clearly, it is extremely difficult for almost anyone to save enough money to pay the exit tax. To make it even worse, the figures above show the fee for *each separate* degree. A person wishing to leave the country must pay the sum of *all* the degrees he has earned, plus a basic "original" fee of 940 rubles ($1175).

Will the Soviets permit large numbers of Jews to leave the country? No one can possibly provide an answer to this question. But several things have become clear in recent years. First, the question of Soviet Jewry has become an important one. In fact, it has become so vital to Soviet-American relations that the basis of the new friendship between the two nations may be affected. An article in the March 26, 1973 issue of *Time* Magazine discusses this very point:

> U.S. negotiators warned the Soviets last May that the preferred tariff treatment they sought would need approval by a finicky Congress. But in August, Moscow began levying its now celebrated 'education tax' on would-be emigrants. . .
>
> House Ways and Means Committee Chairman Wilber Mills, a leader of the exit-tax foes, bluntly told visiting Soviet Deputy Foreign Trade Minister V.S. Alkhimov in Washington last week that Moscow would not get Most Favored Nation [treatment] until the exit tax was dropped. In the Senate, [Senator Henry] Jackson now has lined up 73 co-sponsors for his amendment. It was not just a Jewish issue, he said in a Senate speech, but 'an American issue in this nation of immigrants. . . ! '

The Most Favored Nation clause, referred to in the above article, means that a country's goods can be imported into the United States at the lowest tariff rates in effect for any nation at the present time. This agreement is certainly a most important one to the Russians. Perhaps this situation will enable the Congress of the United States to play a role in making exit from the USSR a possibility for thousands of Jews.

A second answer that has emerged to the question of the Soviet Union's allowing Jews to leave the country is visible in the small numbers of Soviet Jews who have been granted exit visas recently.

A third potential answer is visible in the current firm stand being taken by Soviet Jewry itself. It should be remembered that no oppressor has ever listened to a people who were unwilling to stand up and be counted among the ranks of those opposed to the government's policies. This lesson is apparently very clear to the Jews of Russia. Most of them are not prepared to continue along the road of silence and despair, for they realize that it leads nowhere.

Perhaps this very idea, which hints at the direction which Soviet Jewry will follow in the future, has best been expressed in the following excerpt from an article written by a visitor to the Soviet Union, which appeared in *The New York Times.*

> I walked down a quiet Moscow side street with a gray-haired scientist, a man whose books are on the shelves of every good university library in America. "My wife is only half-Jewish," he said, "and when she registered it was as a Ukrainian. This was common in those days. Fewer of the young

people will do it today. She lived like this until a few years ago, vaguely uncomfortable but not doing anything about it. Then came those terrible days of tension at the end of May, 1967, when we thought that Israel might be annihilated. The violence and style of the official propaganda against Israel was such that we feared it would awake old feelings of anti-Semitism and that our fate too might be hanging in the balance. This was, no doubt, exaggerated, but we felt it and decided that however we were physically isolated from Israel and its troubles, we had to do something to demonstrate our spiritual identification and faith in the future of the Jews.

"My wife went to the militia station and asked to have her nationality registration changed to Jewish. The duty officer scoffed at her and when she insisted, brusquely ordered her out of the station. She stood her ground and demanded to see the station commandant. A little confused at her persistence, the officer led her into the commandant and came out scratching his head and musing aloud, 'Wants to change from Ukrainian to Yid! First time in my life that I've ever seen anyone ask to change a plus to a minus!' That's the way they look at it," my friend concluded. "Nobody in authority in this country has any understanding of why a Jew should want to be a Jew."

Jewish history must be viewed not in years, nor in decades, but in centuries. The Jews of Russia, in the past, have experienced cultural greatness, economic power, merciless persecution and ethnic humiliation. Many times in their history intolerance has driven them to mass migration. Yet one theme persists in their story: the will to survive. It is impossible to predict at this time what the conclusion of this story will be. But one thing is clear. A people who have given so much to the world are worthy of the world's support in their struggle to retain their identity.

A Chronology of the Jews in Russia

YEAR	EVENTS
100 C.E. (approximately)	First Jewish settlements in Russia, on the northern shore of the Black Sea.
Eighth century	Khazars of central Russia adopt Judaism.
Late tenth century	Rise of Kievan Russia.
980	Vladimir, prince of Kiev, adopts Greek Orthodox Christianity as the official religion of Russia.
Thirteenth century	Moscow replaces Kiev as the center of Russian civilization. During this time the Judaizers, led originally by Zechariah, are formed; they are strongly opposed by the Russian Church.

Sixteenth century (approx. 1550) — Many Jews are forced to convert to Christianity.

Mid-seventeenth century — Tsar Alexei brutally persecutes the Jews of Poland, and forces countless Russian Jews out of Russia.

1682–1725 — Peter the Great rules Russia. He feels that Russia is not yet ready for the Jews.

1727 — The Jews of Russia are formally banished from the country and forced to flee to eastern Europe.

1742 — Tsarina Elizabeth expels those few Jews remaining in Russia.

1796 — Catherine the Great successfully conquers all of Poland, thereby bringing thousands of Jews under Russian control once more.

1803 — Minister Speransky advocates freedom for Russia's Jews as a means of using their talents and abilities for the benefit of the Russian Empire.
At about the same time, however, Jews are officially restricted to certain sections of western Russia, known as the "Pale of Settlement."

1816   Tsar Nicholas I blames many problems of the peasantry on the "Zhids" (Jews), and advocates a policy of "Orthodoxy, Autocracy, and Nationality."

1870s   Many Jews join the Populists, a revolutionary group which sought the support of the peasants. However, the peasantry hated the Jews more than it did its own oppressed state. Many peasants turned against the Jewish Populists.

1903   The terrible pogrom of Kishinev.
At this same time, politically active Jews were joining a variety of groups: the Zionists, the Workers' Bund, the Mensheviks and the Bolsheviks.

1913   Joseph Stalin, a Bolshevik, writes "Marxism and the National Question," an essay which details the Marxist-Bolshevik approach to the "Jewish Question."

1914–1918   World War I.

Feb. 1917   The First Russian Revolution. Tsar Nicholas II is deposed and Kerensky comes to power at the head of a Provisional Government.

Oct. 1917   The Second Revolution. The Bolsheviks, under Lenin, successfully overthrow Kerensky's government.

1918–1920   The Soviet Civil War. Jews encounter anti-Semitic treatment at the hands of both the Soviet forces and the "Whites" (pro-tsarist forces).

Early 1920s   The Yevektsiia (Jewish Section of the Communist Party) wages a campaign to stamp out Jewish religious practices in the Soviet Union.

Jan. 1924   Vladimir Ilyich Lenin dies. He is succeeded by a "troika" consisting of Stalin, Zinoviev, and Kamenev. In the following months, Stalin is able to overcome the influence of Kamenev, Zinoviev and his arch rival – Leon Trotsky – by emphasizing the Jewish background of all three men.

1928   Migration of Soviet Jews to the eastern Siberian settlement of Biro-Bidzhan begins with 654 "pioneers."

1929–39   The "Iron Age" of the Soviet Union. During this period collectivization took place on the farms, industrialization

138

developed in the cities, and Soviet culture made great advances.

Mid-1930s   A strenuous anti-religion program is conducted by the government. The Jewish religion is a prime target of this campaign.

1934   The infamous "purges" begin with allegations of involvement in the assassination of Secretary Kirov, a murder which many now believe was planned by Stalin himself.

1939   The Soviet-German Anti-Aggression Pact is signed. Thousands of Polish Jews come under Soviet control.

Summer, 1941   Hitler breaks his promise and invades the Soviet Union.

1941–45   The overwhelming majority of Soviet Jewry is murdered at the hands of the Nazi invaders. Very few Jews are evacuated from the threatened areas by the Soviet authorities before the Germans arrive.

1942   The Jewish Anti-Fascist Committee is established to harness the support of

Western Jewry behind the Soviet war effort.

1945

World War II ends. The Soviet Union, along with the other allied nations, is victorious.

Jan. 1948

Solomon Mikhoels, chairman of the Anti-Fascist Committee is mysteriously murdered. Following this incident, most of the JAC leadership is arrested and executed on charges of treason, stemming from an alleged plan to establish a separate Jewish state in the Crimea.

Late 1952

The "Prague Trials" take place in Czechoslovakia. Many Jews are charged with "Zionism and other crimes against the State."

Spring, 1953

The so-called Doctor's Plot is announced. It was charged that a group of Kremlin doctors had conspired to murder high-ranking Soviet officials. Nearly all of the doctors were Jewish. This was followed by a series of charges in the press against "Jewish conspirators" uncovered throughout the country.

1953

Joseph Vissarionovich Stalin dies. After a period of competition for the ruling

	position in the country, Nikita Khrush-chev emerges as the undisputed leader.
1964	Khrushchev falls from power and is succeeded by Chairman Leonid Brezhnev.
1968–present	Jewish activism grows in protest against anti-Jewish policies in the Soviet Union.
June, 1970	Eleven Jews attempt, unsuccessfully, to hijack a Soviet airplane. They are put on trial and given severe sentences. At the same time, a considerable amount of activism appears among American Jews.
1971	Jews are required to pay an "Exit Tax," determined partly by the extent of their education, in order to leave the Soviet Union.

Suggested Readings

Abramsky, C. "The Biro Bidzhan Project, 1927-1959," in Lionel Kochan, *The Jews in Soviet Russia Since 1917.* London: Oxford University Press, 1970.

Aleichem, Sholom. *Tevye's Daughters.* New York: Crown Publishers, 1949.

Ami, Ben. *Between Hammer and Sickle.* Philadelphia: The Jewish Publication Society, 1967.

Anders, Wladyslaw. *Hitler's Defeat in Russia.* Chicago: Regnery, 1953.

Babel, Isaac. *The Collected Stories of Isaac Babel.* New York: The World Publishing Co., 1966.

Baron, Salo. *The Russian Jews Under Tsars and Soviets.* New York: MacMillan, 1964.

Ben-Gurion, David. *Memoirs.* New York: The World Publishing Co., 1970.

Brodsky, Joseph. "A Jewish Cemetery," in A. Brumberg, ed., *In Quest of Justice.* New York: Praeger, 1970.

Carr, Edward. *The Bolshevik Revolution,* vol. I. New York: MacMillan, 1968.

Cohen, Elliot, ed. *The New Red Anti-Semitism.* Boston: Beacon, 1953.

Conquest, Robert. *The Great Terror.* New York: MacMillan, 1968.

Crossman, Richard, ed. *The God That Failed.* New York: Harper and Row, 1963.

Dennon, Leo. *Where the Ghetto Ends.* New York: Alfred King, 1934.

Deutscher, Isaac. *The Non-Jewish Jew and Other Essays.* London: Oxford University Press, 1968.

Gilboa, Yehoshua. *The Black Years of Soviet Jewry.* Boston: Little, Brown and Co., 1971.

Goldberg, B.Z. *The Jewish Problem in the Soviet Union.* New York: Crown, 1961.

Goldberg, David. *Sussman Sees It Through.* New York: Bloch Publishing, 1935.

Goldhagen, Erich, ed. *Ethnic Minorities in the Soviet Union.* New York: Praeger, 1968.

————, "Communism and Anti-Semitism," in A. Brumberg, *Russia Under Khrushchev.* New York: Praeger, 1962.

Korey, William. *The Soviet Cage: Anti-Semitism in Russia.* New York: The Viking Press, 1973.

Khrushchev, Nikita. *Khrushchev Remembers.* Boston: Little, Brown and Co., 1970.

Kuznetsov, A. *Babi Yar.* New York: Dial Press, 1967.

Labin, Suzanne. *Stalin's Russia.* London: Victor Gollancz, Ltd. 1949.

Lendvai, Paul. *Anti-Semitism Without Jews.* Garden City: Doubleday and Co., 1971.

Litvinoff, Barnett. *To The House of their Fathers.* New York. Praeger, 1965.

Marshall, Richard, Bird, Thomas, Blane, Andrew, eds. *Aspects of Religion in the Soviet Union, 1917-1967.* Chicago: University of Chicago Press, 1971.

McSherry, James. *Stalin, Hitler and Europe.* New York: The World Publishing Co., 1968.

Meyer, Peter, ed. *The Jews in the Soviet Satellites.* Syracuse: University of Syracuse Press, 1953.

Nedova, Joseph. *Trotsky and the Jews.* Philadelphia: The Jewish Publication Society of America, 1971.

Poliakov, Leon. *The History of Anti-Semitism,* vol. I. New York: The Vanguard Press, Inc., 1965.

Rothenberg, Joshua. "Jewish Religion in the Soviet Union," in Kochan, op. cit.

Rubin, Ronald, ed. *The Unredeemed: Anti-Semitism in the Soviet Union.* Chicago: Quadrangle Books, 1968.

Schechtman, Joseph. *Star in Eclipse.* New York: Thomas Yoseloff, 1961.

Schmelz, Uziel, comp. *Jewish Demography and Statistics.* Jerusalem: Hebrew University Press, 1961.

Schuman, Frederick. *Government in the Soviet Union.* New York: Thomas Y. Crowell Co., 1961.

Schwarz, Solomon. *The Jews in the Soviet Union.* Syracuse: University of Syracuse Press, 1951.

Smolar, Joseph. *Soviet Jewry Today and Tomorrow.* New York: MacMillan, 1971.

Stalin, Joseph. *Marxism and the National Question.* Moscow: Foreign Language Publishing House, 1947.

Teller, Judd. *The Kremlin, the Jews and the Middle East.* New York: Thomas Yoseloff, 1957.

Trotsky, Leon. *Stalin.* New York: Stein and Day, 1967.

————. *The Basic Writings of Trotsky,* ed. Irving Howe. New York: Random House, 1963.

145

Ulam, R. *The Bolsheviks.* New York: MacMillan, 1965.

Wiesel, Elie. *The Jews of Silence.* New York: Holt, Rinehart and Winston, 1966.

PAMPHLETS, JOURNALS AND PERIODICALS

Ainsztein, Reuben. "The War Record of Soviet Jewry," *Jewish Social Studies.* January, 1966, pp. 3-24.

Aronson, Gregory, Browder, Earl, Lyons, Eugene, Samuel, Maurice. "Reflections on Stalinist anti-Semitism," *Midstream.* Spring, 1957.

———. "Communist Anti-Semitism." Report to Jewish Labor Committee Conference. April 18, 1953.

———. "Soviet Russia and the Jews." New York: American Jewish League Against Communism, 1949.

Glassman, Leo. "Soviet Russia's Jews," *B'nai Brith Magazine.* July-August, 1930, pp. 386-89.

Goldstein, Anatole. "The Attitude of the Recent Russian Emigrés Toward the Jewish Question." New York: Institute of Jewish Affairs, 1952.

Greenbaum, Alfred. "Soviet Jewry During the Lenin-Stalin Period," *Soviet Studies.* April, 1965, pp. 406-21.

Kroll, M.A. "The Jews in Soviet Russia," *B'nai Brith Magazine.* March, 1930, pp. 232-33.

London, Isaac. "Days of Anxiety: A Chapter in the History of Soviet Jewry," *Jewish Social Studies.* July-October, 1953, pp. 275-93.

Redlich, Shimon. "The Jewish Anti-Fascist Committee in the Soviet Union," *Jewish Social Studies.* January, 1969, pp. 25-36.

Roeh, Nirah. "Is Russian Jewry Doomed?" *Contemporary Russia.* 1938, pp. 427-41.

Sherman, C.B. "Forty Years of the Soviet Pogrom," *Midstream.* Autumn, 1956, pp. 74-83.

Current Digest of the Soviet Press.

Index to *The New York Times* (See: USSR; Jews)

Readers' Guide to Periodical Literature (See: USSR; Jews)